Christmas Cheer

MAD LIBS®

MW00892714

MAD LIBS
An Imprint of Penguin Random House LLC, New York

Mad Libs format and text copyright © 1985, 2001, 2005, 2010, 2018, 2019
by Penguin Random House LLC. All rights reserved.

Concept created by Roger Price & Leonard Stern

Photo credit: cover, throughout interior: felt texture: Eshma/iStock/Getty Images Plus

Christmas Cheer Mad Libs published in 2019 by Mad Libs,
an imprint of Penguin Random House LLC, New York.
Manufactured in China.

Visit us online at www.penguinrandomhouse.com.

Penguin supports copyright. Copyright fuels creativity, encourages diverse voices,
promotes free speech, and creates a vibrant culture. Thank you for buying an authorized
edition of this book and for complying with copyright laws by not reproducing,
scanning, or distributing any part of it in any form without permission. You are
supporting writers and allowing Penguin to continue to publish books for every reader.

Christmas Cheer Mad Libs ISBN 9781524793388

3 5 7 9 10 8 6 4

MAD LIBS is a registered trademark of Penguin Random House LLC.

MAD LIBS®

STOCKING STUFFER
MAD LIBS

by Leigh Olsen

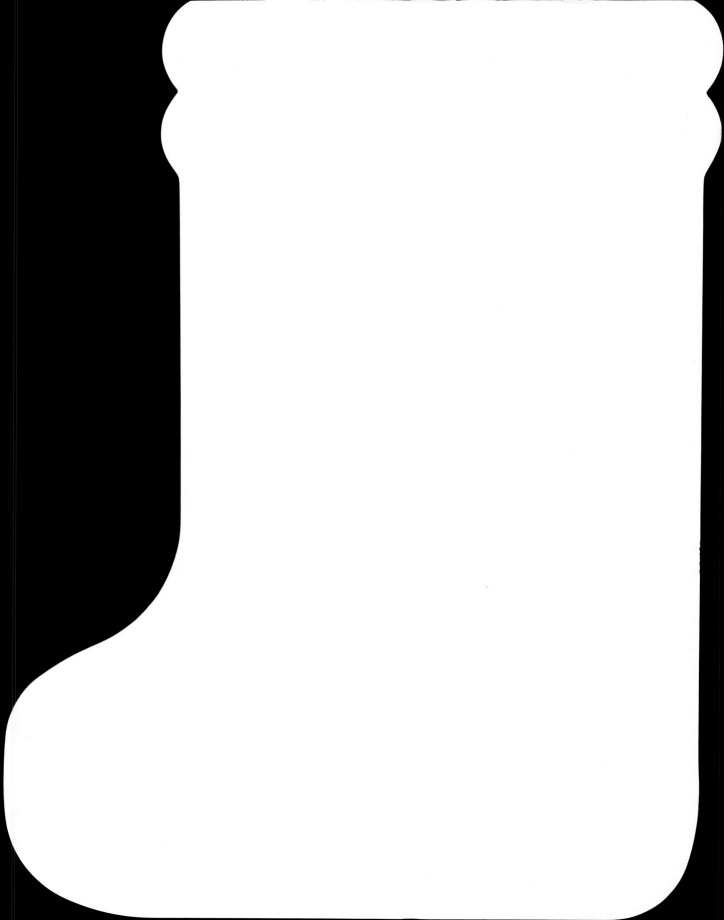

INSTRUCTIONS

MAD LIBS® is a game for people who don't like games!
It can be played by one, two, three, four, or forty.

• RIDICULOUSLY SIMPLE DIRECTIONS

In this tablet you will find stories containing blank spaces where words
are left out. One player, the READER, selects one of these stories. The
READER does not tell anyone what the story is about. Instead, he/she asks
the other players, the WRITERS, to give him/her words. These words are
used to fill in the blank spaces in the story.

• TO PLAY

The READER asks each WRITER in turn to call out a word—an adjective or
a noun or whatever the space calls for—and uses them to fill in the blank
spaces in the story. The result is a MAD LIBS® game.

When the READER then reads the completed MAD LIBS® game to the other
players, they will discover that they have written a story that is fantastic,
screamingly funny, shocking, silly, crazy, or just plain dumb—depending
upon which words each WRITER called out.

• EXAMPLE (*Before* and *After*)

" _____ !" he said _____
           EXCLAMATION   ADVERB

as he jumped into his convertible _____ and
                                              NOUN

drove off with his _____ wife.
                           ADJECTIVE

"   OUCH   !" he said   STUPIDLY
           EXCLAMATION   ADVERB

as he jumped into his convertible   CAT   and
                                              NOUN

drove off with his   BRAVE   wife.
                           ADJECTIVE

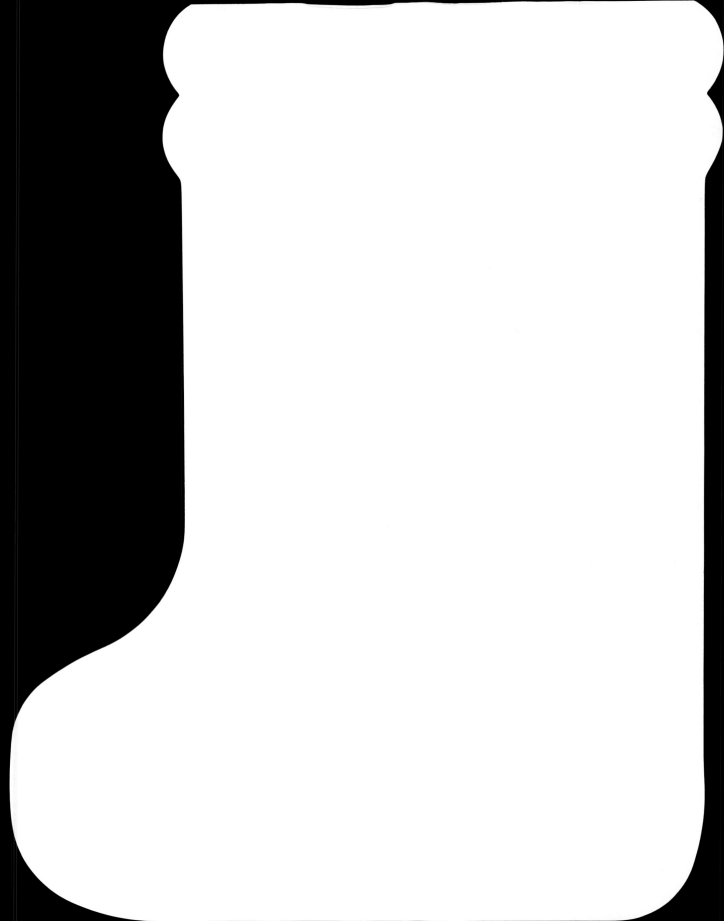

QUICK REVIEW

In case you have forgotten what adjectives, adverbs, nouns, and verbs are, here is a quick review:

An ADJECTIVE describes something or somebody. *Lumpy*, *soft*, *ugly*, *messy*, and *short* are adjectives.

An ADVERB tells how something is done. It modifies a verb and usually ends in "ly." *Modestly*, *stupidly*, *greedily*, and *carefully* are adverbs.

A NOUN is the name of a person, place, or thing. *Sidewalk*, *umbrella*, *bridle*, *bathtub*, and *nose* are nouns.

A VERB is an action word. *Run*, *pitch*, *jump*, and *swim* are verbs. Put the verbs in past tense if the directions say PAST TENSE. *Ran*, *pitched*, *jumped*, and *swam* are verbs in the past tense.

When we ask for A PLACE, we mean any sort of place: a country or city (*Spain*, *Cleveland*) or a room (*bathroom*, *kitchen*).

An EXCLAMATION or SILLY WORD is any sort of funny sound, gasp, grunt, or outcry, like *Wow!*, *Ouch!*, *Whomp!*, *Ick!*, and *Gadzooks!*

When we ask for specific words, like a NUMBER, a COLOR, an ANIMAL, or a PART OF THE BODY, we mean a word that is one of those things, like *seven*, *blue*, *horse*, or *head*.

When we ask for a PLURAL, it means more than one. For example, *cat* pluralized is *cats*.

SANTA CLAUS IS COMING

VERB _____

A PLACE _____

NOUN _____

ADJECTIVE _____

NOUN _____

ADJECTIVE _____

NOUN _____

PLURAL NOUN _____

VERB _____

PLURAL NOUN _____

PART OF THE BODY _____

PLURAL NOUN _____

PLURAL NOUN _____

TYPE OF LIQUID _____

TYPE OF FOOD _____

NOUN _____

MAD LIBS® is fun to play with friends, but you can also play it by yourself! To begin with, DO NOT look at the story on the page below. Fill in the blanks on this page with the words called for. Then, using the words you have selected, fill in the blank spaces in the story.

Now you've created your own hilarious MAD LIBS® game!

SANTA CLAUS IS COMING

You better watch out and you better not _____, because Santa

_____VERB

Claus is coming to (the) _____! Santa hails from the frigid

_____A PLACE

North _____, where he lives with his _____ wife,

_____NOUN_____ADJECTIVE

Mrs. Claus. Santa runs a magical _____ workshop where

_____NOUN

_____ elves build every kind of toy you can imagine, from

ADJECTIVE

_____ trucks to wooden _____ to baby dolls that

___NOUN_____PLURAL NOUN

_____ when you tickle them! On Christmas Eve, Santa loads

VERB

up his sleigh, which is pulled by eight flying _____ plus

_____PLURAL NOUN

one reindeer named Rudolph who has a shiny red _____ to

_____PART OF THE BODY

light the way. Then Santa and his reindeer fly around the world,

bringing _____ to good little girls and _____.

_____PLURAL NOUN_____PLURAL NOUN

If you leave him cookies and _____, he'll eat them happily!

_____TYPE OF LIQUID

"Ho, ho, ho!" he'll laugh, and his belly will shake like a bowlful of

_____. "Merry Christmas to all, and to all a good

TYPE OF FOOD

_____!"

NOUN

From STOCKING STUFFER MAD LIBS® • Copyright © 2018 by Penguin Random House LLC.

MAD LIBS® is fun to play with friends, but you can also play it by yourself! To begin with, DO NOT look at the story on the page below. Fill in the blanks on this page with the words called for. Then, using the words you have selected, fill in the blank spaces in the story.

Now you've created your own hilarious MAD LIBS® game!

DEAR DIARY

VERB _____

PART OF THE BODY (PLURAL) _____

ARTICLE OF CLOTHING _____

VERB _____

ADJECTIVE _____

PART OF THE BODY (PLURAL) _____

VEHICLE _____

ADJECTIVE _____

PLURAL NOUN _____

ADJECTIVE _____

VERB _____

ADJECTIVE _____

NOUN _____

ADVERB _____

DEAR DIARY

Ho, ho, ho, diary! Christmas is only a few weeks away, and I'm so

excited, I could _____! The elves have been working their
                        VERB

_____ off to get all the toys ready in time. Mrs.
PART OF THE BODY (PLURAL)

Claus has made sure my red-and-white _____ is in
                                        ARTICLE OF CLOTHING

pristine condition. And the reindeer are ready to _____!
                                                    VERB

Christmas is the most _____ time of the year. I love bringing
                        ADJECTIVE

joy to the _____ of children around the world. Yes,
            PART OF THE BODY (PLURAL)

it's a lot of work flying around the globe in a/an _____ in
                                                    VEHICLE

just one night, but it's a/an _____ thrill. (And I love the milk
                                ADJECTIVE

and _____ kids leave me, too!) I've still got some work to
        PLURAL NOUN

do before the _____ day arrives. I've made my list, but I still
                ADJECTIVE

have to _____ it twice to find out who has been naughty or
        VERB

_____. I hope I don't have to put coal in anyone's _____!
ADJECTIVE   NOUN

Yours _____,
        ADVERB

Santa Claus

From STOCKING STUFFER MAD LIBS® • Copyright © 2018 by Penguin Random House LLC.

MAD LIBS® is fun to play with friends, but you can also play it by yourself! To begin with, DO NOT look at the story on the page below. Fill in the blanks on this page with the words called for. Then, using the words you have selected, fill in the blank spaces in the story.

Now you've created your own hilarious MAD LIBS® game!

A LETTER TO SANTA

A PLACE _____

NOUN _____

NOUN _____

NOUN _____

A PLACE _____

NOUN _____

PLURAL NOUN _____

ADJECTIVE _____

NOUN _____

ADJECTIVE _____

PART OF THE BODY _____

PLURAL NOUN _____

ADVERB _____

PERSON IN ROOM _____

A LETTER TO SANTA

Dear Santa,

Greetings from (the) _____! I am so excited for you to visit
<u>A PLACE</u>

my house, come down my chimney, and put presents under the

Christmas _____! I have been a very good little _____
<u>NOUN</u> <u>NOUN</u>

this year. I made my bed, put the dishes in the _____, and
<u>NOUN</u>

even took the garbage to (the) _____! My mom says she is as
<u>A PLACE</u>

proud as a/an _____. She says she's also proud of me because
<u>NOUN</u>

I learned how to ride a bike without any training _____!
<u>PLURAL NOUN</u>

Since I've been so good this year, _____ Santa, I was
<u>ADJECTIVE</u>

wondering—could I please have a brand-new shiny red ten-speed

_____ for Christmas this year? I promise to take _____
<u>NOUN</u> <u>ADJECTIVE</u>

care of it, and to always wear a helmet on my _____ when I
<u>PART OF THE BODY</u>

ride it. Thanks, Santa! I'll be sure to leave you extra milk and

_____ this year.
<u>PLURAL NOUN</u>

_____,
<u>ADVERB</u>

_____
<u>PERSON IN ROOM</u>

From STOCKING STUFFER MAD LIBS® • Copyright © 2018 by Penguin Random House LLC.

MAD LIBS® is fun to play with friends, but you can also play it by yourself! To begin with, DO NOT look at the story on the page below. Fill in the blanks on this page with the words called for. Then, using the words you have selected, fill in the blank spaces in the story.

Now you've created your own hilarious MAD LIBS® game!

VISIT THE NORTH POLE

PLURAL NOUN _____

NOUN _____

ARTICLE OF CLOTHING _____

NUMBER _____

PART OF THE BODY (PLURAL) _____

ADJECTIVE _____

PLURAL NOUN _____

ANIMAL (PLURAL) _____

ADJECTIVE _____

NOUN _____

ADVERB _____

PLURAL NOUN _____

CELEBRITY _____

NOUN _____

NOUN _____

VISIT THE NORTH POLE

Looking for the perfect vacation spot to relax and throw all your

_____ away? Hop on a/an _____ and come to the
<u>PLURAL NOUN</u>   <u>NOUN</u>

North Pole! Be sure to pack your warmest _____.
                                          <u>ARTICLE OF CLOTHING</u>

The average temperature in the summer is freezing, and in the winter,

it's a balmy negative _____ degrees! Get ready to feast your
                       <u>NUMBER</u>

_____ on all the _____ wildlife. The
<u>PART OF THE BODY (PLURAL)</u>   <u>ADJECTIVE</u>

North Pole has everything from seals to polar _____ to
                                               <u>PLURAL NOUN</u>

arctic _____! Reindeer live here, too, of course—
       <u>ANIMAL (PLURAL)</u>

although you'll only find the flying kind at Santa's _____
                                                     <u>ADJECTIVE</u>

workshop. If you're lucky, perhaps you'll stumble upon this magical

_____. Ask _____, and one of the elves might give
<u>NOUN</u>   <u>ADVERB</u>

you a tour! It's a working factory, so all the elves will be tinkering away

making _____. But perhaps you'll see _____ and
       <u>PLURAL NOUN</u>   <u>CELEBRITY</u>

can blurt out what you'd like under your Christmas _____!
                                                   <u>NOUN</u>

Don't delay—book your flight to the North _____ today!
                                           <u>NOUN</u>

From STOCKING STUFFER MAD LIBS® • Copyright © 2018 by Penguin Random House LLC.

MAD LIBS® is fun to play with friends, but you can also play it by yourself! To begin with, DO NOT look at the story on the page below. Fill in the blanks on this page with the words called for. Then, using the words you have selected, fill in the blank spaces in the story.

Now you've created your own hilarious MAD LIBS® game!

MEET THE ELVES

VERB _____

ADJECTIVE _____

PERSON IN ROOM _____

NOUN _____

VEHICLE (PLURAL) _____

PLURAL NOUN _____

PERSON IN ROOM _____

PLURAL NOUN _____

A PLACE _____

CELEBRITY _____

SAME CELEBRITY _____

SAME CELEBRITY _____

NOUN _____

PLURAL NOUN _____

NOUN _____

PERSON IN ROOM _____

VERB _____

EXCLAMATION _____

MEET THE ELVES

Who exactly are the elves who _____ in Santa's workshop?

VERB

All elves are as friendly as can be, and they each have their own

_____ talents!

ADJECTIVE

- _____ the Elf is a master _____ whittler and

PERSON IN ROOM   NOUN

  specializes in carving wooden cars and _____, wooden

VEHICLE (PLURAL)

  blocks, and wooden _____.

PLURAL NOUN

- _____ knits soft, warm socks, sweaters, and

PERSON IN ROOM

  _____. Some say they're the coziest clothes in (the)

PLURAL NOUN

  _____!

A PLACE

- _____ the Elf (not to be confused with the famous

CELEBRITY

  _____) specializes in sporting equipment. _____

SAME CELEBRITY   SAME CELEBRITY

  the Elf makes everything from _____ balls to hockey

NOUN

  _____ and _____ rackets!

PLURAL NOUN   NOUN

- _____ the Elf makes lifelike dolls that _____

PERSON IN ROOM   VERB

  when you hug them! _____!

EXCLAMATION

From STOCKING STUFFER MAD LIBS® • Copyright © 2018 by Penguin Random House LLC.

MAD LIBS® is fun to play with friends, but you can also play it by yourself! To begin with, DO NOT look at the story on the page below. Fill in the blanks on this page with the words called for. Then, using the words you have selected, fill in the blank spaces in the story.

Now you've created your own hilarious MAD LIBS® game!

SANTA FACTS

NOUN _____

ADJECTIVE _____

COLOR _____

PART OF THE BODY _____

PERSON IN ROOM _____

PLURAL NOUN _____

VERB ENDING IN "S" _____

NOUN _____

VERB ENDING IN "ING" _____

SANTA FACTS

Do you know everything there is to know about that jolly old

_____ named Santa Claus? Here are some _____ facts!
    NOUN   ADJECTIVE

- Santa has a/an _____ beard on his _____.
                      COLOR   PART OF THE BODY

- Santa's favorite reindeer is _____.
                                  PERSON IN ROOM

- Santa's sleigh is powered by fairy _____.
                                      PLURAL NOUN

- To get inside your house on Christmas Eve, Santa _____
                                                    VERB ENDING IN "S"

  down the chimney.

- Santa's favorite cookie is _____ chip.
                                NOUN

- In the off-season, Santa's favorite hobby is _____
                                                    VERB ENDING IN "ING"

  with Mrs. Claus.

From STOCKING STUFFER MAD LIBS® • Copyright © 2018 by Penguin Random House LLC.

SANTA AROUND THE WORLD

NOUN _____

PLURAL NOUN _____

NOUN _____

ADJECTIVE _____

PART OF THE BODY (PLURAL) _____

NOUN _____

PLURAL NOUN _____

NOUN _____

PERSON IN ROOM _____

PLURAL NOUN _____

ADJECTIVE _____

NOUN _____

A PLACE _____

PLURAL NOUN _____

MAD LIBS® is fun to play with friends, but you can also play it by yourself! To begin with, DO NOT look at the story on the page below. Fill in the blanks on this page with the words called for. Then, using the words you have selected, fill in the blank spaces in the story.

Now you've created your own hilarious MAD LIBS® game!

SANTA AROUND
THE WORLD

Because Santa Claus is a magical _____, not many _____
 NOUN   PLURAL NOUN
know what he's *really* like. Here are some unique ways children around

the _____ imagine Santa Claus:
     NOUN

• In Japan, children believe Santa is a/an _____ monk
                                              ADJECTIVE
  named Hotei-osho, who has _____ on the back
                             PART OF THE BODY (PLURAL)
  of his head.

• In Italy, La Befana is a friendly witch who flies on a/an _____
                                                              NOUN
  and leaves candies, figs, and _____ in children's socks.
                                 PLURAL NOUN

• In Russia, Santa is called Grandfather _____, and he
                                          NOUN
  brings his granddaughter, _____, with him when
                             PERSON IN ROOM
  he delivers _____ to children.
              PLURAL NOUN

• In Sweden, Santa is jolly and fat with a/an _____ beard,
                                               ADJECTIVE
  but he is also very tiny—some say he's barely the size of a/an

  _____!
  NOUN

• In the Netherlands, children call Santa "Sinterklaas," and they

  believe he lives in (the) _____ and that he takes a whole
                            A PLACE
  three weeks to deliver _____.
                         PLURAL NOUN

From STOCKING STUFFER MAD LIBS® • Copyright © 2018 by Penguin Random House LLC.

UP CLOSE AND PERSONAL WITH MRS. CLAUS

PERSON IN ROOM _____

ADJECTIVE _____

VERB ENDING IN "ING" _____

ADJECTIVE _____

NOUN _____

NOUN _____

PLURAL NOUN _____

NOUN _____

PLURAL NOUN _____

ADJECTIVE _____

NOUN _____

NOUN _____

NOUN _____

PART OF THE BODY _____

MAD LIBS® is fun to play with friends, but you can also play it by yourself! To begin with, DO NOT look at the story on the page below. Fill in the blanks on this page with the words called for. Then, using the words you have selected, fill in the blank spaces in the story.

Now you've created your own hilarious MAD LIBS® game!

UP CLOSE AND PERSONAL
WITH MRS. CLAUS

The following is an excerpt from a rare interview between TV

personality _____ and the _____ Mrs. Claus:
      PERSON IN ROOM   ADJECTIVE

Interviewer: Mrs. Claus, thank you for _____ with me.
                                          VERB ENDING IN "ING"

People know a lot about your _____ husband, Santa Claus, but
                              ADJECTIVE

to many, you remain a/an _____ of mystery. Who *is* Mrs. Claus?
                          NOUN

Mrs. Claus: I'm just your average, ordinary _____! Yes, I
                                                 NOUN

admit, I am excellent at baking _____. I enjoy running the
                                 PLURAL NOUN

_____ workshop with Santa. And I love caring for our nine
   NOUN

flying _____.
        PLURAL NOUN

Interviewer: Who really runs the show, you or your _____
                                                       ADJECTIVE

husband?

Mrs. Claus: I'm more of a behind-the-scenes _____. Santa is
                                                 NOUN

the star of the _____!
                 NOUN

Interviewer: Fair enough. What's it like being married to Santa?

Mrs. Claus: Wonderful! He is my best _____, and I love him
                                          NOUN

with all of my _____!
                PART OF THE BODY

From STOCKING STUFFER MAD LIBS® • Copyright © 2018 by Penguin Random House LLC.

MAD LIBS® is fun to play with friends, but you can also play it by yourself! To begin with, DO NOT look at the story on the page below. Fill in the blanks on this page with the words called for. Then, using the words you have selected, fill in the blank spaces in the story.

Now you've created your own hilarious MAD LIBS® game!

SANTA'S FAVORITE COOKIES

ADJECTIVE _____

NOUN _____

NOUN _____

NOUN _____

ADJECTIVE _____

ANIMAL _____

TYPE OF LIQUID _____

ADVERB _____

VERB _____

ADVERB _____

PLURAL NOUN _____

PLURAL NOUN _____

ADJECTIVE _____

PLURAL NOUN _____

PLURAL NOUN _____

NOUN _____

SANTA'S FAVORITE COOKIES

Here is Mrs. Claus's recipe for _____ cookies!

ADJECTIVE

Preheat your _____ to 375 degrees. In a large bowl, combine

NOUN

one cup of _____, a teaspoon of _____, and a/an

NOUN   NOUN

_____ teaspoon of salt. In another bowl, crack one _____

ADJECTIVE   ANIMAL

egg and add a teaspoon of _____. Beat _____.

TYPE OF LIQUID   ADVERB

Then, combine all the ingredients and _____. Chill the

VERB

dough, roll it out _____, and use cookie cutters to make

ADVERB

festive shapes such as Christmas _____ and holiday

PLURAL NOUN

_____. Bake until the cookies are _____. Allow

PLURAL NOUN   ADJECTIVE

them to cool, and then decorate them with sprinkles, icing, and

_____. And now for the best part—eat as many _____

PLURAL NOUN   PLURAL NOUN

as you like! Just be sure to save a few for _____ Claus!

NOUN

From STOCKING STUFFER MAD LIBS® • Copyright © 2018 by Penguin Random House LLC.

MAD LIBS® is fun to play with friends, but you can also play it by yourself! To begin with, DO NOT look at the story on the page below. Fill in the blanks on this page with the words called for. Then, using the words you have selected, fill in the blank spaces in the story.

Now you've created your own hilarious MAD LIBS® game!

ANOTHER LETTER TO SANTA

NOUN _____

ADJECTIVE _____

NOUN _____

PLURAL NOUN _____

SAME PLURAL NOUN _____

SILLY WORD _____

VERB ENDING IN "ING" _____

PERSON IN ROOM _____

NOUN _____

NOUN _____

SAME NOUN _____

SAME NOUN _____

ADJECTIVE _____

NOUN _____

PLURAL NOUN _____

NOUN _____

ADVERB _____

PERSON IN ROOM _____

ANOTHER LETTER TO SANTA

Dear Santa,

I've been an okay _____ this year. I was good sometimes, and
                         NOUN

I wasn't so _____ other times. I got decent grades in school,
            ADJECTIVE

but I almost never cleaned my _____. I brushed my _____
                      NOUN   PLURAL NOUN

every day, but I never flossed my _____. I was nice to my
                                  SAME PLURAL NOUN

mom and dad, except for that time I got mad and yelled, "_____"
                                              SILLY WORD

because they wouldn't let me go bungee _____ with
                                  VERB ENDING IN "ING"

_____. You catch my _____. I've been a so-so
PERSON IN ROOM   NOUN

_____, a mediocre _____, a rather average
     NOUN   SAME NOUN

_____. So, _____ Santa, I've decided to be realistic
 SAME NOUN   ADJECTIVE

this year and ask you for just one small _____ under the
                                      NOUN

Christmas tree. I'd really like a book about _____. That's all.
                                        PLURAL NOUN

And I promise, I'll try to be a really, really good _____ next year.
                                          NOUN

Yours _____,
      ADVERB

_____
PERSON IN ROOM

From STOCKING STUFFER MAD LIBS® • Copyright © 2018 by Penguin Random House LLC.

FLYING REINDEER 101

EXCLAMATION _____

ADJECTIVE _____

NOUN _____

PLURAL NOUN _____

ADJECTIVE _____

NOUN _____

A PLACE _____

A PLACE _____

NOUN _____

NUMBER _____

NUMBER _____

PART OF THE BODY _____

PLURAL NOUN _____

NOUN _____

MAD LIBS® is fun to play with friends, but you can also play it by yourself! To begin with, DO NOT look at the story on the page below. Fill in the blanks on this page with the words called for. Then, using the words you have selected, fill in the blank spaces in the story.

Now you've created your own hilarious MAD LIBS® game!

FLYING REINDEER 101

_____! You've just adopted a flying reindeer! Congratulations!
EXCLAMATION

Here are a few _____ tips for taking care of your new _____:
ADJECTIVE   NOUN

• Feed your flying reindeer its fair share of _____ each day.
PLURAL NOUN

• Be sure to keep its fur shiny and _____ by brushing it
ADJECTIVE

  every day with a coarse-bristled _____.
NOUN

• Even though your reindeer can fly from (the) _____ to
A PLACE

  (the) _____, its hooves can still get dirty. Clean its hooves
A PLACE

  with a/an _____.
NOUN

• Your flying reindeer's velvety antlers can grow to be _____
NUMBER

  feet tall and _____ feet wide! They fall out each year, so don't
NUMBER

  be alarmed. It'll grow another pair of antlers on its _____!
PART OF THE BODY

• Finally, give your flying reindeer all the love and _____
PLURAL NOUN

  it deserves, and it will be your _____ for life!
NOUN

From STOCKING STUFFER MAD LIBS® • Copyright © 2018 by Penguin Random House LLC.

MAD LIBS® is fun to play with friends, but you can also play it by yourself! To begin with, DO NOT look at the story on the page below. Fill in the blanks on this page with the words called for. Then, using the words you have selected, fill in the blank spaces in the story.

Now you've created your own hilarious MAD LIBS® game!

SANTA'S WISH LIST

_____ ADJECTIVE

_____ PLURAL NOUN

_____ NOUN

_____ ADJECTIVE

_____ NOUN

_____ ADJECTIVE

_____ NOUN

_____ A PLACE

_____ A PLACE

_____ VERB

_____ PLURAL NOUN

_____ VERB

_____ NOUN

_____ VERB

_____ NOUN

SANTA'S WISH LIST

My _____ wife, Mrs. Claus,
        ADJECTIVE

While most of the _____ around the world send their
                    PLURAL NOUN

Christmas lists to *me*, I am the only lucky _____ who gets to
                                              NOUN

send my Christmas list to *you*, the _____ Mrs. Claus. I was a
                                      ADJECTIVE

very good _____ this year, so I hope you'll get me the one
           NOUN

present I'd really love—going on _____ adventures with you,
                                  ADJECTIVE

my one true _____! We can go camping in (the) _____.
             NOUN   A PLACE

We can take a cruise to (the) _____. We can even stay home
                               A PLACE

and _____ by the fireplace while we read books about
     VERB

_____, or play card games like Go _____ and
  PLURAL NOUN   VERB

Old _____. I don't care where we are or what we do, so long
     NOUN

as I get to _____ with you!
             VERB

Merry Christmas!

Your sweet _____,
            NOUN

Santa

From STOCKING STUFFER MAD LIBS® • Copyright © 2018 by Penguin Random House LLC.

NAUGHTY OR NICE?

NOUN _____

ADJECTIVE _____

NOUN _____

SAME NOUN _____

NOUN _____

NUMBER _____

NOUN _____

PLURAL NOUN _____

SAME PLURAL NOUN _____

PLURAL NOUN _____

NUMBER _____

PERSON IN ROOM _____

NOUN _____

NOUN _____

MAD LIBS® is fun to play with friends, but you can also play it by yourself! To begin with, DO NOT look at the story on the page below. Fill in the blanks on this page with the words called for. Then, using the words you have selected, fill in the blank spaces in the story.

Now you've created your own hilarious MAD LIBS® game!

NAUGHTY OR NICE?

Not sure whether you're on the nice list or the naughty _____?
NOUN

Take this _____ quiz to find out!
ADJECTIVE

1. When your parent asks you to clean up your _____, you
NOUN

   say (a) "Okay!" or (b) "I wouldn't clean up my _____ if I
SAME NOUN

   were the last _____ on earth!"
NOUN

2. When you find _____ dollars on the street, you (a) take it to
NUMBER

   the local _____ station or (b) immediately go to the
NOUN

   _____ store and purchase as many _____
PLURAL NOUN   SAME PLURAL NOUN

   as you can afford.

3. When you have to write an essay about _____ for
PLURAL NOUN

   school, you (a) finish it as soon as you can or (b) watch _____
NUMBER

   hours of reruns of *Judge* _____ on TV instead.
PERSON IN ROOM

If you answered mostly *a*'s, good news! You've been a good

_____ this year. Answered mostly *b*'s? Sorry, Santa might just
NOUN

be bringing you a lump of _____ for Christmas!
NOUN

From STOCKING STUFFER MAD LIBS® • Copyright © 2018 by Penguin Random House LLC.

MAD LIBS® is fun to play with friends, but you can also play it by yourself! To begin with, DO NOT look at the story on the page below. Fill in the blanks on this page with the words called for. Then, using the words you have selected, fill in the blank spaces in the story.

Now you've created your own hilarious MAD LIBS® game!

SANTA GOES TO
HOLLYWOOD

PLURAL NOUN _____

NOUN _____

PERSON IN ROOM _____

NOUN _____

NOUN _____

ADJECTIVE _____

PERSON IN ROOM _____

PLURAL NOUN _____

NOUN _____

PERSON IN ROOM _____

FIRST NAME _____

NOUN _____

ADJECTIVE _____

PERSON IN ROOM _____

SANTA GOES TO HOLLYWOOD

Santa Claus has made his fair share of appearances in big-budget

Hollywood _____. Here are just a few!
         PLURAL NOUN

- In *The Polar* _____, a young child named _____
                   NOUN   PERSON IN ROOM

  takes a/an _____ to the North Pole. When he arrives,
                  NOUN

  Santa gives the little boy the first _____ of Christmas.
                                              NOUN

- In *The Santa Clause*, a dad and his _____ child,
                                              ADJECTIVE

  _____, are magically transported to the North Pole,
       PERSON IN ROOM

  where the dad discovers he has to deliver _____ as the
                                                    PLURAL NOUN

  new Santa on Christmas Eve.

- In _____ *on 34th Street*, the Santa Claus at _____'s
        NOUN   PERSON IN ROOM

  department store, who goes by _____ Kringle, claims
                                       FIRST NAME

  to be the *real* Santa Claus. Is he the real deal or is he a fake

  _____? A/An _____ child named _____
       NOUN   ADJECTIVE   PERSON IN ROOM

  believes him.

From STOCKING STUFFER MAD LIBS® • Copyright © 2018 by Penguin Random House LLC.

SANTA'S WORKOUT ROUTINE

VERB ENDING IN "ING" _____

PLURAL NOUN _____

NOUN _____

ADJECTIVE _____

NOUN _____

PART OF THE BODY (PLURAL) _____

NOUN _____

NOUN _____

NUMBER _____

PLURAL NOUN _____

PART OF THE BODY (PLURAL) _____

ADJECTIVE _____

ADJECTIVE _____

PLURAL NOUN _____

PART OF THE BODY _____

MAD LIBS® is fun to play with friends, but you can also play it by yourself! To begin with, DO NOT look at the story on the page below. Fill in the blanks on this page with the words called for. Then, using the words you have selected, fill in the blank spaces in the story.

Now you've created your own hilarious MAD LIBS® game!

SANTA'S WORKOUT ROUTINE

It's hard work _____ around the world in one night,
       VERB ENDING IN "ING"

not to mention climbing up and down millions of _____
                                                  PLURAL NOUN

to deliver toys! Yes, Santa is a magical _____, but he also
                                           NOUN

needs to stay in shape to make sure he's ready for his _____
                                                        ADJECTIVE

day. Santa Claus has a vigorous exercise _____. First he
                                            NOUN

stretches by reaching to touch his _____. Then he
                                   PART OF THE BODY (PLURAL)

jogs on a/an _____-mill or rides an exercise _____.
             NOUN   NOUN

To make sure he's strong enough to lift heavy presents, he does squats

with _____-pound _____—and this makes his
       NUMBER   PLURAL NOUN

_____ really muscular! All of this _____
PART OF THE BODY (PLURAL)   ADJECTIVE

exercise makes Santa feel _____, and it also allows him to
                            ADJECTIVE

treat himself to milk and _____ whenever he likes. After
                          PLURAL NOUN

all, Santa has to make sure his _____ shakes like a bowlful
                                PART OF THE BODY

of jelly!

From STOCKING STUFFER MAD LIBS® • Copyright © 2018 by Penguin Random House LLC.

MAD LIBS® is fun to play with friends, but you can also play it by yourself! To begin with, DO NOT look at the story on the page below. Fill in the blanks on this page with the words called for. Then, using the words you have selected, fill in the blank spaces in the story.

Now you've created your own hilarious MAD LIBS® game!

SLEIGH MAINTENANCE

PERSON IN ROOM —————————————————

ADJECTIVE —————————————————

NOUN —————————————————

NOUN —————————————————

PLURAL NOUN —————————————————

ADJECTIVE —————————————————

VERB ENDING IN "S" —————————————————

PART OF THE BODY (PLURAL) —————————————————

TYPE OF LIQUID —————————————————

PART OF THE BODY —————————————————

PLURAL NOUN —————————————————

TYPE OF LIQUID —————————————————

ADJECTIVE —————————————————

VERB —————————————————

SLEIGH MAINTENANCE

Hi, there! I'm _____ the Elf. Welcome to Santa's sleigh garage.
<u>PERSON IN ROOM</u>

This is where our _____ team works to make sure the sleigh is
<u>ADJECTIVE</u>

in tip-top shape. It's no ordinary _____ , after all—Santa's
<u>NOUN</u>

sleigh is a work of _____ . It is made with all the latest
<u>NOUN</u>

technology, including the finest lightweight carbon _____ .
<u>PLURAL NOUN</u>

All year long, the elves and I make repairs and improvements to the

sleigh so it's in _____ condition by the time Christmas
<u>ADJECTIVE</u>

_____ around. We wax the runners and polish them
<u>VERB ENDING IN "S"</u>

until we can see our _____ in them. We put on a
<u>PART OF THE BODY (PLURAL)</u>

fresh coat of red _____ . And this year, we even added
<u>TYPE OF LIQUID</u>

special upgrades, like heated seats to warm Santa's _____
<u>PART OF THE BODY</u>

and satellite radio so he can listen to all the best Christmas

_____ while he's driving. We even added a heated cup
<u>PLURAL NOUN</u>

holder to hold a mug of Mrs. Claus's delicious hot _____ .
<u>TYPE OF LIQUID</u>

With that, our _____ job is done, and Santa's sleigh is ready
<u>ADJECTIVE</u>

to _____ !
<u>VERB</u>

From STOCKING STUFFER MAD LIBS® • Copyright © 2018 by Penguin Random House LLC.

SANTA'S SUMMER VACATION

_____ NOUN

_____ NOUN

_____ PART OF THE BODY

_____ ADJECTIVE

_____ VEHICLE

_____ A PLACE

_____ NOUN

_____ NUMBER

_____ EXCLAMATION

_____ ANIMAL (PLURAL)

_____ PLURAL NOUN

_____ PLURAL NOUN

_____ PART OF THE BODY (PLURAL)

_____ NOUN

_____ ADJECTIVE

_____ NOUN

_____ NOUN

MAD LIBS® is fun to play with friends, but you can also play it by yourself! To begin with, DO NOT look at the story on the page below. Fill in the blanks on this page with the words called for. Then, using the words you have selected, fill in the blank spaces in the story.

Now you've created your own hilarious MAD LIBS® game!

SANTA'S SUMMER VACATION

All year long, the North _____ is wintry and cold, and big wet
                            NOUN

_____-flakes fall from the sky. Sometimes, I need a break to
NOUN

warm my _____! That's why Mrs. Claus and I go on a/an
         PART OF THE BODY

_____ summer vacation each year. This year, we hopped in
ADJECTIVE

a/an _____ and traveled to (the) sunny _____. We
     VEHICLE   A PLACE

stayed in a four-star _____ right on the beach! We took surfing
                      NOUN

lessons and learned to hang _____ while yelling, "_____!"
                            NUMBER   EXCLAMATION

We swam in the ocean with _____. We ate local
                          ANIMAL (PLURAL)

_____, relaxed, read books about _____, and
PLURAL NOUN   PLURAL NOUN

let the sun shine on our _____. It was just what the
                         PART OF THE BODY (PLURAL)

_____ ordered! We came home to the _____ Pole
NOUN   ADJECTIVE

feeling rested and rejuvenated, and ready to face the _____
                                                      NOUN

and get back to work. After all, Christmas is just around the

_____!
NOUN

From STOCKING STUFFER MAD LIBS® • Copyright © 2018 by Penguin Random House LLC.

HOW DOES HE DO IT?

VERB ENDING IN "S" _____

NOUN _____

NOUN _____

PLURAL NOUN _____

VERB _____

NOUN _____

PLURAL NOUN _____

ADJECTIVE _____

NOUN _____

PLURAL NOUN _____

NOUN _____

EXCLAMATION _____

CELEBRITY _____

PLURAL NOUN _____

ADJECTIVE _____

PLURAL NOUN _____

PLURAL NOUN _____

NOUN _____

MAD LIBS® is fun to play with friends, but you can also play it by yourself! To begin with, DO NOT look at the story on the page below. Fill in the blanks on this page with the words called for. Then, using the words you have selected, fill in the blank spaces in the story.

Now you've created your own hilarious MAD LIBS® game!

HOW DOES HE DO IT?

Santa _____ around the world in one night. But how?
      VERB ENDING IN "S"

We have the inside _____! Unnamed sources inside Santa's
            NOUN

workshop tell us Santa is a magical _____. It's true! He can
                  NOUN

put millions of _____ into his sack of toys. He shrinks
          PLURAL NOUN

himself to _____ down chimneys. And he bends time and
          VERB

_____ to visit millions of _____ on Christmas
NOUN   PLURAL NOUN

Eve. Santa's _____ sleigh is *also* magical. Said one anonymous
          ADJECTIVE

_____ inside the workshop, "Whether there's wind or snow or
NOUN

_____ falling from the sky, the sleigh can travel at the speed
PLURAL NOUN

of _____!" _____! Then there are the reindeer—
   NOUN   EXCLAMATION

Dasher, Dancer, Prancer, Vixen, Comet, Cupid, Donner, Blitzen, and

_____. They are also magical. They can fly like _____
CELEBRITY   PLURAL NOUN

through the sky! So, there you have it—the _____ secret to
                            ADJECTIVE

how Santa delivers _____ to all the world's _____,
              PLURAL NOUN   PLURAL NOUN

finally revealed for all the _____ to see. It's magic!
                  NOUN

From STOCKING STUFFER MAD LIBS® • Copyright © 2018 by Penguin Random House LLC.

ONE MORE LETTER TO SANTA

NOUN _____

LAST NAME _____

NOUN _____

PLURAL NOUN _____

PERSON IN ROOM _____

PLURAL NOUN _____

EXCLAMATION _____

VERB _____

PLURAL NOUN _____

ADJECTIVE _____

PART OF THE BODY (PLURAL) _____

ADJECTIVE _____

NOUN _____

NUMBER _____

LETTER OF THE ALPHABET _____

PERSON IN ROOM _____

MAD LIBS® is fun to play with friends, but you can also play it by yourself! To begin with, DO NOT look at the story on the page below. Fill in the blanks on this page with the words called for. Then, using the words you have selected, fill in the blank spaces in the story.

Now you've created your own hilarious MAD LIBS® game!

ONE MORE LETTER
TO SANTA

Dear Santa,

I am very sorry. I was a very bad _____ this year. I talked
 NOUN

during all of Mrs. _____'s lessons. I never did my
 LAST NAME

_____ homework. And I passed notes about _____
NOUN PLURAL NOUN

to _____ all day long. And that's just at school! At home, I
PERSON IN ROOM

never listened to my _____. They would ask me to clean
 PLURAL NOUN

up after dinner, and I'd shout, "_____!" and _____
 EXCLAMATION VERB

in my bedroom instead. My bedroom floor was covered in

_____, and my bed was _____. I rarely took a
PLURAL NOUN ADJECTIVE

bath or brushed my _____. I smelled _____!
 PART OF THE BODY (PLURAL) ADJECTIVE

Santa, I'm very sorry I was such a naughty _____. I promise
 NOUN

I'll be better next year. But I'd like to know, can I have a brand-new

_____-thousand-dollar _____-Phone for
NUMBER LETTER OF THE ALPHABET

Christmas, anyway? Thanks!

From,

_____
PERSON IN ROOM

From STOCKING STUFFER MAD LIBS® • Copyright © 2018 by Penguin Random House LLC.

MAD LIBS® is fun to play with friends, but you can also play it by yourself! To begin with, DO NOT look at the story on the page below. Fill in the blanks on this page with the words called for. Then, using the words you have selected, fill in the blank spaces in the story.

Now you've created your own hilarious MAD LIBS® game!

THE NAUGHTY LIST

ADJECTIVE _____

PLURAL NOUN _____

ADJECTIVE _____

PERSON IN ROOM _____

SILLY WORD _____

VERB (PAST TENSE) _____

CELEBRITY _____

VERB _____

PERSON IN ROOM _____

NOUN _____

PERSON IN ROOM _____

VERB ENDING IN "ING" _____

ADVERB _____

CELEBRITY _____

NOUN _____

ANIMAL _____

PERSON IN ROOM _____

NOUN _____

THE NAUGHTY LIST

Here is a list of some of the _____ children who will be getting
 ADJECTIVE

coal in their _____ this year and their most _____
 PLURAL NOUN   ADJECTIVE

offenses:

- _____ called the family dog a/an _____ after he
 PERSON IN ROOM   SILLY WORD

  _____ in the house.
  VERB (PAST TENSE)

- _____ refused to listen when asked to _____
 CELEBRITY   VERB

  the table for dinner.

- _____ cut in line while waiting to be served mystery
 PERSON IN ROOM

  _____ in the school cafeteria.
  NOUN

- _____ got detention for _____
 PERSON IN ROOM   VERB ENDING IN "ING"

  _____ in the middle of class.
  ADVERB

- _____ cheated during a game of Pin the _____
 CELEBRITY   NOUN

  on the _____.
  ANIMAL

- _____ ate a dirty _____ off the floor . . . twice!
 PERSON IN ROOM   NOUN

From STOCKING STUFFER MAD LIBS® • Copyright © 2018 by Penguin Random House LLC.

MAD LIBS® is fun to play with friends, but you can also play it by yourself! To begin with, DO NOT look at the story on the page below. Fill in the blanks on this page with the words called for. Then, using the words you have selected, fill in the blank spaces in the story.

Now you've created your own hilarious MAD LIBS® game!

SANTA SIGHTING

PLURAL NOUN _____

A PLACE _____

PART OF THE BODY _____

NOUN _____

PLURAL NOUN _____

PERSON IN ROOM _____

PLURAL NOUN _____

NOUN _____

PART OF THE BODY (PLURAL) _____

PLURAL NOUN _____

NOUN _____

PLURAL NOUN _____

ADVERB _____

NOUN _____

PLURAL NOUN _____

ADJECTIVE _____

VERB _____

PLURAL NOUN _____

SANTA SIGHTING

Attention! Breaking _____! It's Christmas Eve, and Santa
<u>PLURAL NOUN</u>

is believed to have been spotted in (the) _____. According to
<u>A PLACE</u>

a/an _____-witness, he was riding his magic _____
<u>PART OF THE BODY</u>   <u>NOUN</u>

with his flying _____ leading the way. The witness, a child
<u>PLURAL NOUN</u>

named _____, recalls, "As soon as I saw him, I yelled, 'Oh my
<u>PERSON IN ROOM</u>

_____, it's _____ Claus!' I could not believe my
<u>PLURAL NOUN</u>   <u>NOUN</u>

_____." According to the child, Santa and his
<u>PART OF THE BODY (PLURAL)</u>

_____ landed on top of a/an _____. Santa
<u>PLURAL NOUN</u>   <u>NOUN</u>

climbed out of the sleigh with his sack full of _____ and
<u>PLURAL NOUN</u>

quickly disappeared down the chimney while the reindeer waited

_____. "Before long, Santa came back out, and the next thing I
<u>ADVERB</u>

knew, jolly old St. _____ and his sleigh were landing on *my*
<u>NOUN</u>

house! I heard the reindeer's _____ on my roof. Isn't that
<u>PLURAL NOUN</u>

the most _____ thing you've ever heard? I am so excited for
<u>ADJECTIVE</u>

Christmas morning, I could just _____!" There you have it, folks!
<u>VERB</u>

Santa's here in town, and he's delivering _____ to *you* next!
<u>PLURAL NOUN</u>

From STOCKING STUFFER MAD LIBS® • Copyright © 2018 by Penguin Random House LLC.

HAPPILY EVER
MAD LIBS

by Roger Price & Leonard Stern

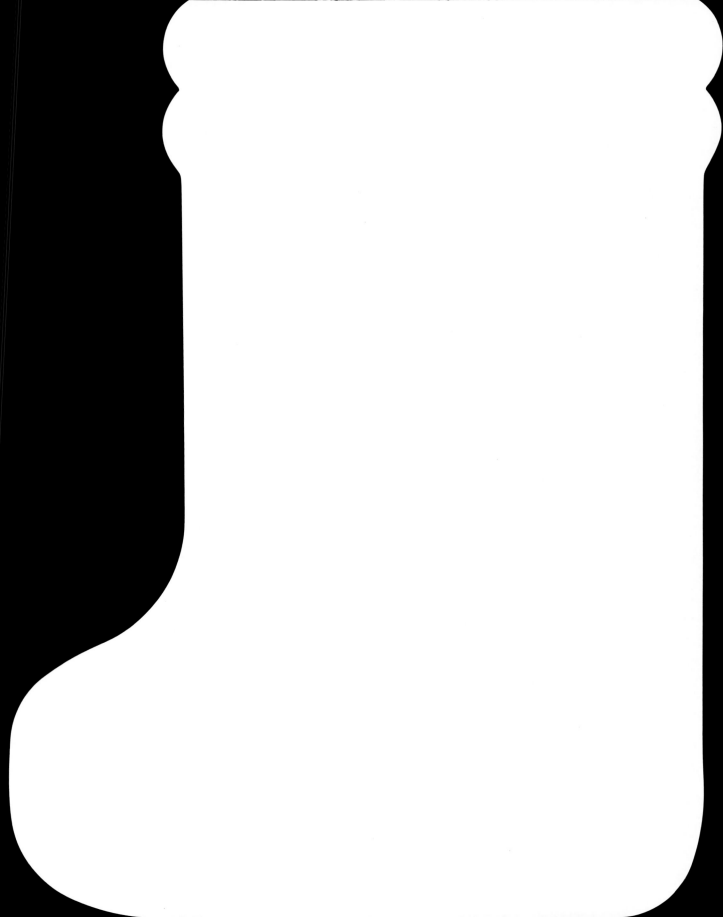

INSTRUCTIONS

MAD LIBS® is a game for people who don't like games!
It can be played by one, two, three, four, or forty.

● RIDICULOUSLY SIMPLE DIRECTIONS

In this tablet you will find stories containing blank spaces where words
are left out. One player, the READER, selects one of these stories. The
READER does not tell anyone what the story is about. Instead, he/she asks
the other players, the WRITERS, to give him/her words. These words are
used to fill in the blank spaces in the story.

● TO PLAY

The READER asks each WRITER in turn to call out a word—an adjective or
a noun or whatever the space calls for—and uses them to fill in the blank
spaces in the story. The result is a MAD LIBS® game.

When the READER then reads the completed MAD LIBS® game to the other
players, they will discover that they have written a story that is fantastic,
screamingly funny, shocking, silly, crazy, or just plain dumb—depending
upon which words each WRITER called out.

● EXAMPLE (*Before* and *After*)

"_____!" he said _____
　　　　EXCLAMATION　　　　　　　　　　　　　ADVERB

as he jumped into his convertible _____ and
　　　　　　　　　　　　　　　　　　　　　NOUN

drove off with his _____ wife.
　　　　　　　　　ADJECTIVE

"_____OUCH_____!" he said ____STUPIDLY____
　　　　EXCLAMATION　　　　　　　　　　　　　ADVERB

as he jumped into his convertible _____CAT_____ and
　　　　　　　　　　　　　　　　　　　　　NOUN

drove off with his ____BRAVE____ wife.
　　　　　　　　　ADJECTIVE

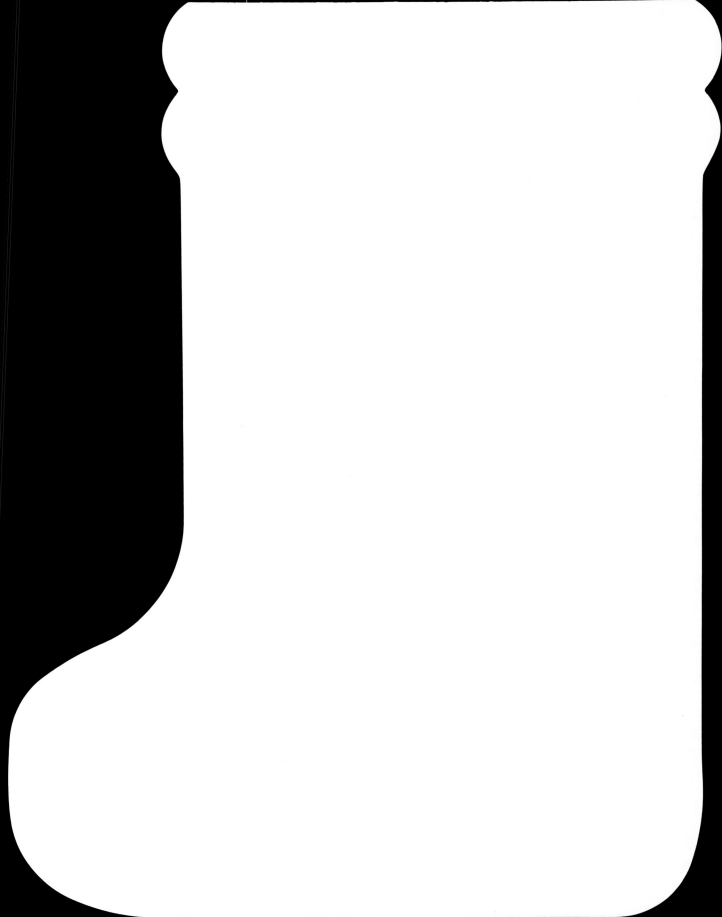

QUICK REVIEW

In case you have forgotten what adjectives, adverbs, nouns, and verbs are, here is a quick review:

An ADJECTIVE describes something or somebody. *Lumpy*, *soft*, *ugly*, *messy*, and *short* are adjectives.

An ADVERB tells how something is done. It modifies a verb and usually ends in "ly." *Modestly*, *stupidly*, *greedily*, and *carefully* are adverbs.

A NOUN is the name of a person, place, or thing. *Sidewalk*, *umbrella*, *bridle*, *bathtub*, and *nose* are nouns.

A VERB is an action word. *Run*, *pitch*, *jump*, and *swim* are verbs. Put the verbs in past tense if the directions say PAST TENSE. *Ran*, *pitched*, *jumped*, and *swam* are verbs in the past tense.

When we ask for A PLACE, we mean any sort of place: a country or city (*Spain*, *Cleveland*) or a room (*bathroom*, *kitchen*).

An EXCLAMATION or SILLY WORD is any sort of funny sound, gasp, grunt, or outcry, like *Wow!*, *Ouch!*, *Whomp!*, *Ick!*, and *Gadzooks!*

When we ask for specific words, like a NUMBER, a COLOR, an ANIMAL, or a PART OF THE BODY, we mean a word that is one of those things, like *seven*, *blue*, *horse*, or *head*.

When we ask for a PLURAL, it means more than one. For example, *cat* pluralized is *cats*.

MAD LIBS® is fun to play with friends, but you can also play it by yourself! To begin with, DO NOT look at the story on the page below. Fill in the blanks on this page with the words called for. Then, using the words you have selected, fill in the blank spaces in the story.

Now you've created your own hilarious MAD LIBS® game!

JACK AND THE BEANSTALK

NOUN _____

NOUN _____

PERSON IN ROOM _____

PLURAL NOUN _____

ADJECTIVE _____

NOUN _____

PART OF THE BODY (PLURAL) _____

ADJECTIVE _____

ADJECTIVE _____

SILLY WORD _____

PLURAL NOUN _____

NUMBER _____

JACK AND THE BEANSTALK

Once upon a time, there was a/an _____ named Jack who
_{NOUN}
lived with his mother in a tiny _____. The only thing they
NOUN
owned was a cow named _____. Jack's mom told him to
PERSON IN ROOM
sell the cow to buy some _____. On his way to the market,
PLURAL NOUN
Jack met a stranger who said, "I'll trade you these _____
ADJECTIVE
beans for your cow." Jack agreed, but when his mom learned he had
disobeyed her, she was angrier than a wild _____ and
NOUN
threw the beans out the window. As they slept, the beans grew into
a gigantic beanstalk. When Jack awoke, he couldn't believe
his _____. He immediately climbed the
PART OF THE BODY (PLURAL)
_____ beanstalk. At the top, he met a/an _____
ADJECTIVE   ADJECTIVE
giant. "Fee, fi, fo, _____!" the angry giant bellowed. Jack
SILLY WORD
quickly escaped, grabbing a hen that laid golden _____,
PLURAL NOUN
and quickly climbed down the beanstalk. With their newfound wealth,
Jack and his mother bought _____ cows and lived happily
NUMBER
ever after.

From HAPPILY EVER MAD LIBS® • Copyright © 2010 by Penguin Random House LLC.

MAD LIBS® is fun to play with friends, but you can also play it by yourself! To begin with, DO NOT look at the story on the page below. Fill in the blanks on this page with the words called for. Then, using the words you have selected, fill in the blank spaces in the story.

Now you've created your own hilarious MAD LIBS® game!

LIVE WITH HANSEL AND GRETEL

ADJECTIVE ———————————————

PLURAL NOUN ———————————————

ADJECTIVE ———————————————

ADJECTIVE ———————————————

PLURAL NOUN ———————————————

PLURAL NOUN ———————————————

ADJECTIVE ———————————————

NOUN ———————————————

PLURAL NOUN ———————————————

NOUN ———————————————

ADJECTIVE ———————————————

CELEBRITY ———————————————

LIVE WITH HANSEL AND GRETEL

The following is a/an _____ interview to be read aloud by
ADJECTIVE

three _____ :
PLURAL NOUN

Host: Welcome to *Fairy Tale Forum*. We're here live with the

_____ Hansel and Gretel. Gretel, tell us what happened.
ADJECTIVE

Gretel: Well, our _____ stepmother kept taking us into the
ADJECTIVE

woods so we'd get lost.

Hansel: But I left a trail of _____ so we could find our way back.
PLURAL NOUN

Host: But then something unexpected happened, right?

Gretel: Yes. We found a house made entirely of candy _____ .
PLURAL NOUN

Hansel: And we were so _____ that we started to eat it. But
ADJECTIVE

then a witch popped out and put me in a/an _____ .
NOUN

Host: Oh, my _____ ! How did you escape?
PLURAL NOUN

Hansel: Gretel pushed the witch into a/an _____ and we
NOUN

ran home.

Host: What a/an _____ story. Viewers, join us next
ADJECTIVE

time when we find out if Prince Charming is secretly dating

_____ .
CELEBRITY

From HAPPILY EVER MAD LIBS® • Copyright © 2010 by Penguin Random House LLC.

MAD LIBS® is fun to play with friends, but you can also play it by yourself! To begin with, DO NOT look at the story on the page below. Fill in the blanks on this page with the words called for. Then, using the words you have selected, fill in the blank spaces in the story.

Now you've created your own hilarious MAD LIBS® game!

THE WOLF'S SIDE
OF THE STORY

_____ ADJECTIVE

_____ VERB ENDING IN "ING"

_____ ADJECTIVE

_____ NOUN

_____ PART OF THE BODY (PLURAL)

_____ PLURAL NOUN

_____ NOUN

_____ NOUN

_____ PLURAL NOUN

_____ PART OF THE BODY (PLURAL)

_____ ADJECTIVE

_____ NOUN

_____ ADJECTIVE

_____ ADJECTIVE

THE WOLF'S SIDE
OF THE STORY

I am the big, _____ wolf. You may have heard the lies Little
            ADJECTIVE

Red _____ Hood has told about me. But now it's my
    VERB ENDING IN "ING"

turn to tell you the truth. One day, Little Red Riding Hood was on her

way to visit her _____ grandmother. But I happened to get
       ADJECTIVE

there first. I knocked, but there was no answer. Then I remembered it

was Wednesday and Grandma would be at her weekly _____
                               NOUN

game. I'd been on my _____ all day, so I decided to
       PART OF THE BODY (PLURAL)

let myself in to take a nap. It was freezing in the house, so I slipped

into one of Grandma's _____ and fell into a deep
        PLURAL NOUN

_____. I was awakened by Little Red Riding
 NOUN

_____ shouting at me, saying insulting things like
 NOUN

"What big _____ you have!" and "What big
       PLURAL NOUN

_____ you have." Offended, I got up and left.
PART OF THE BODY (PLURAL)

Believe me, that's the _____ truth and nothing but the
         ADJECTIVE

_____. So, you see, I'm not the _____ fiend
 NOUN   ADJECTIVE

Little Red makes me out to be. I'm the real victim in this

_____ tale!
 ADJECTIVE

From HAPPILY EVER MAD LIBS® • Copyright © 2010 by Penguin Random House LLC.

CASTLE FOR SALE

_____ OCCUPATION

_____ ADJECTIVE

_____ ADJECTIVE

_____ PERSON IN ROOM

_____ ADJECTIVE

_____ ADJECTIVE

_____ A PLACE

_____ ADJECTIVE

_____ PART OF THE BODY

_____ PART OF THE BODY

_____ PLURAL NOUN

_____ NOUN

_____ ADVERB

_____ NOUN

_____ VERB

_____ ADJECTIVE

_____ PLURAL NOUN

_____ PLURAL NOUN

_____ ADJECTIVE

_____ NUMBER

MAD LIBS® is fun to play with friends, but you can also play it by yourself. To begin with, DO NOT look at the story on the page below. Fill in the blanks on this page with the words called for. Then, using the words you have selected, fill in the blank spaces in the story.

Now you've created your own hilarious MAD LIBS® game!

CASTLE FOR SALE

Are you a king, queen, or _____ looking for that perfectly
                                OCCUPATION

_____ new home? Then have we got a/an _____
ADJECTIVE   ADJECTIVE

place for you! King _____'s _____ castle has
                     PERSON IN ROOM   ADJECTIVE

just come on the market! Originally built in the _____ Ages,
                                                   ADJECTIVE

this lakefront wonder has towers that rise high above (the)

_____ and a/an _____ view that will take your
A PLACE   ADJECTIVE

_____ away. In each and every room of this 25,000-square-
PART OF THE BODY

_____ masterpiece, there are magnificent stained glass
PART OF THE BODY

_____ and splendid Gothic _____-burning
PLURAL NOUN   NOUN

fireplaces. There's also a chef's state-of-the-art, _____ modern
                                                     ADVERB

_____ for those who love to _____. For security
NOUN   VERB

and _____ privacy, there is also a moat filled with
     ADJECTIVE

_____ and a drawbridge to keep out unwanted
PLURAL NOUN

_____. Take advantage of the collapse in the castle market
PLURAL NOUN

and make a/an _____ offer on this treasure. The asking price
               ADJECTIVE

is a ridiculously low _____ dollars.
                       NUMBER

From HAPPILY EVER MAD LIBS® • Copyright © 2010 by Penguin Random House LLC.

CINDERELLA

ADJECTIVE _____

ADJECTIVE _____

ADJECTIVE _____

PART OF THE BODY _____

NOUN _____

ADJECTIVE _____

NOUN _____

NOUN _____

NOUN _____

NOUN _____

PLURAL NOUN _____

PERSON IN ROOM _____

PLURAL NOUN _____

PART OF THE BODY _____

ADVERB _____

MAD LIBS® is fun to play with friends, but you can also play it by yourself! To begin with, DO NOT look at the story on the page below. Fill in the blanks on this page with the words called for. Then, using the words you have selected, fill in the blank spaces in the story.

Now you've created your own hilarious MAD LIBS® game!

CINDERELLA

There once was a/an _____ young girl named Cinderella who
_____ADJECTIVE_____

lived with her _____ stepmother and two _____
_____ADJECTIVE_____ _____ADJECTIVE_____

stepsisters. She waited on them hand and _____, but they
_____PART OF THE BODY_____

treated her like a/an _____. Cinderella heard about a ball the
_____NOUN_____

prince was throwing, but she didn't have a/an _____ gown to
_____ADJECTIVE_____

wear. Then, out of the clear blue _____, her fairy _____
_____NOUN_____ _____NOUN_____

-mother appeared and waved her magic _____. Cinderella's
_____NOUN_____

ragged clothes turned into a beautiful _____, and her worn
_____NOUN_____

work shoes became a pair of glass _____. Cinderella went to
_____PLURAL NOUN_____

the ball and danced with Prince _____, who fell madly in
_____PERSON IN ROOM_____

love with her. But at the stroke of midnight she had to flee, losing one of

her glass _____. The prince traveled throughout the
_____PLURAL NOUN_____

kingdom, trying the slipper on the _____ of every young
_____PART OF THE BODY_____

girl, but, of course, it fit only one—Cinderella! The two were soon

married and lived _____ ever after.
_____ADVERB_____

From HAPPILY EVER MAD LIBS® • Copyright © 2010 by Penguin Random House LLC.

MAD LIBS® is fun to play with friends, but you can also play it by yourself! To begin with, DO NOT look at the story on the page below. Fill in the blanks on this page with the words called for. Then, using the words you have selected, fill in the blank spaces in the story.

Now you've created your own hilarious MAD LIBS® game!

PRINCESS SEEKING FAIRY GODMOTHER

ADJECTIVE _____

PERSON IN ROOM _____

ADJECTIVE _____

ADJECTIVE _____

NUMBER _____

ADJECTIVE _____

PLURAL NOUN _____

NOUN _____

PLURAL NOUN _____

PLURAL NOUN _____

PLURAL NOUN _____

PLURAL NOUN _____

VERB ENDING IN "ING" _____

ADJECTIVE _____

PLURAL NOUN _____

PLURAL NOUN _____

PART OF THE BODY (PLURAL) _____

ADVERB _____

PRINCESS SEEKING
FAIRY GODMOTHER

Wanted: One _____ godmother needed immediately for
                        ADJECTIVE

_____ , a very _____ young princess
      PERSON IN ROOM   ADJECTIVE

with a/an _____ personality. Applicant must have
              ADJECTIVE

at least _____ years of _____ experience helping
              NUMBER   ADJECTIVE

princesses or other royal _____ live up to their
                              PLURAL NOUN

_____ and making their _____ come true. The
      NOUN   PLURAL NOUN

ideal candidate should be able to turn pumpkins into _____
                                                          PLURAL NOUN

and mice into _____ who are capable of pulling oversized
                  PLURAL NOUN

_____ . Since the princess enjoys ballroom _____
   PLURAL NOUN   VERB ENDING IN "ING"

with _____ princes, expertise in waltzes, polkas, and
          ADJECTIVE

_____ is a must. Salary will be paid in golden _____
   PLURAL NOUN   PLURAL NOUN

—as many as you can carry in your _____ . Please
                                      PART OF THE BODY (PLURAL)

apply as _____ as possible!
              ADVERB

From HAPPILY EVER MAD LIBS® • Copyright © 2010 by Penguin Random House LLC.

MAD LIBS® is fun to play with friends, but you can also play it by yourself! To begin with, DO NOT look at the story on the page below. Fill in the blanks on this page with the words called for. Then, using the words you have selected, fill in the blank spaces in the story.

Now you've created your own hilarious MAD LIBS® game!

FROM A SPELL BOOK
FOR WICKED QUEENS

_____ ADJECTIVE

_____ ADJECTIVE

_____ ADJECTIVE

_____ ADJECTIVE

_____ TYPE OF LIQUID

_____ NOUN

_____ NUMBER

_____ PART OF THE BODY

_____ NUMBER

_____ ADJECTIVE

_____ PART OF THE BODY

_____ NOUN

_____ NOUN

_____ ADJECTIVE

_____ ADJECTIVE

_____ ADJECTIVE

_____ ADJECTIVE

FROM A SPELL BOOK
FOR WICKED QUEENS

Need to make a/an _____ princess fall into a deep,
                        ADJECTIVE

_____ sleep? Here is a recipe that will bring incredibly
  ADJECTIVE

_____ results. First, put a large _____ cauldron,
  ADJECTIVE   ADJECTIVE

filled to the brim with _____ , on an open _____
                          TYPE OF LIQUID   NOUN

and heat to _____ degrees. When it begins to boil, add
               NUMBER

a/an _____ from a newt and _____ freshly
       PART OF THE BODY   NUMBER

caught _____ lizards. Mash them up well and mix with the
         ADJECTIVE

_____ of a toad and the _____ of a small, furry
  PART OF THE BODY   NOUN

_____ . Once again, bring to a/an _____ boil.
  NOUN   ADJECTIVE

Now you can offer the brew to any unsuspecting _____
                                                    ADJECTIVE

princess. They fall for it every time. But beware: No matter how strong

the _____ potion is, true love will reverse its _____
      ADJECTIVE   ADJECTIVE

spell every time!

From HAPPILY EVER MAD LIBS® • Copyright © 2010 by Penguin Random House LLC.

MAD LIBS® is fun to play with friends, but you can also play it by yourself! To begin with, DO NOT look at the story on the page below. Fill in the blanks on this page with the words called for. Then, using the words you have selected, fill in the blank spaces in the story.

Now you've created your own hilarious MAD LIBS® game!

THE THREE
BILLY GOATS GRUFF

_____ ADJECTIVE

_____ ADJECTIVE

_____ ADJECTIVE

_____ NOUN

_____ VERB

_____ NOUN

_____ NOUN

_____ ADJECTIVE

_____ NOUN

_____ ADVERB

_____ EXCLAMATION

_____ NOUN

_____ NOUN

THE THREE
BILLY GOATS GRUFF

Once there were three _____ billy goats with the last name
                          ADJECTIVE

of Gruff. They wanted to cross a river to eat the _____ grass
                                                    ADJECTIVE

on the other side. But the bridge was guarded by a fearsome,

_____ troll who devoured any _____ who tried to
ADJECTIVE   NOUN

cross it. When the first and littlest billy goat started to

_____ over the bridge, the terrifying _____
     VERB   NOUN

shouted, "I'm going to eat you!" Thinking fast on his _____,
                                                          NOUN

the billy goat said, "Wait, I have a brother who is bigger and more

_____ than I am. You can eat him." So the troll waited for
 ADJECTIVE

the next billy _____ . When he appeared, the same thing
                   NOUN

happened. So the troll waited _____ for the third and
                                  ADVERB

biggest billy goat. This time the troll jumped out and cried,

"_____ ! I am going to eat you!" But the biggest billy goat
  EXCLAMATION

simply lifted the troll with his horns and knocked him into the raging

_____ below. From then on, the billy goats feasted in the
   NOUN

fields on the other side of the _____ to their hearts' content.
                                    NOUN

From HAPPILY EVER MAD LIBS® • Copyright © 2010 by Penguin Random House LLC.

MAD LIBS® is fun to play with friends, but you can also play it by yourself! To begin with, DO NOT look at the story on the page below. Fill in the blanks on this page with the words called for. Then, using the words you have selected, fill in the blank spaces in the story.

Now you've created your own hilarious MAD LIBS® game!

RECIPE FOR THE
BEST PORRIDGE EVER

_____ PERSON IN ROOM

_____ PLURAL NOUN

_____ ADJECTIVE

_____ NOUN

_____ ADJECTIVE

_____ ADJECTIVE

_____ PLURAL NOUN

_____ ADJECTIVE

_____ PLURAL NOUN

_____ NUMBER

_____ NOUN

_____ ADJECTIVE

_____ PLURAL NOUN

_____ ADJECTIVE

_____ ADJECTIVE

_____ NOUN

_____ PLURAL NOUN

RECIPE FOR THE
BEST PORRIDGE EVER

Hi. I'm _____, but you probably know me as
          PERSON IN ROOM

Mama Bear from "Goldilocks and the Three _____." I'm
                                              PLURAL NOUN

here to tell you about making incredibly _____ porridge.
                                              ADJECTIVE

Lots of folks say that eating my porridge is even better than eating a

juicy sirloin _____. To make really _____
                  NOUN   ADJECTIVE

porridge, you start by filling a/an _____ pot with water.
                                        ADJECTIVE

Then add two cups of oats, a few chopped _____, and
                                              PLURAL NOUN

plenty of _____ _____. Place the pot on the
              ADJECTIVE   PLURAL NOUN

stove for _____ hours. Stir with a/an _____ so it
              NUMBER   NOUN

will be nice and _____. This recipe should amply serve
                      ADJECTIVE

three bears or fifty-three _____. Now, some like it
                                PLURAL NOUN

_____, some like it _____, and some like it just
  ADJECTIVE   ADJECTIVE

right. And, by the way, unless you plan to share this porridge,

be on the lookout for _____-stealing girls named
                          NOUN

Goldi-_____.
          PLURAL NOUN

From HAPPILY EVER MAD LIBS® • Copyright © 2010 by Penguin Random House LLC.

RUMPELSTILTSKIN

OCCUPATION _____

ADJECTIVE _____

NOUN _____

ADJECTIVE _____

PART OF THE BODY _____

PLURAL NOUN _____

NOUN _____

NOUN _____

ADVERB _____

ADJECTIVE _____

PART OF THE BODY (PLURAL) _____

ADJECTIVE _____

MAD LIBS® is fun to play with friends, but you can also play it by yourself! To begin with, DO NOT look at the story on the page below. Fill in the blanks on this page with the words called for. Then, using the words you have selected, fill in the blank spaces in the story.

Now you've created your own hilarious MAD LIBS® game!

RUMPELSTILTSKIN

There once was a greedy _____ who said that his daughter
　　　　　　　　　　　　　　OCCUPATION

could spin straw into gold. The _____ king put the girl in a
　　　　　　　　　　　　　　　ADJECTIVE

room filled with straw and gave her until the _____ rose to
　　　　　　　　　　　　　　　　　　　　　NOUN

prove herself. She knew she wasn't capable of such a feat, but at

midnight, a/an _____ man appeared. "I'll turn the straw into
　　　　　　　ADJECTIVE

gold if you give me the necklace around your _____," he
　　　　　　　　　　　　　　　　　　　　PART OF THE BODY

said. She did, and the room filled with golden _____. The
　　　　　　　　　　　　　　　　　　　　　PLURAL NOUN

same thing happened the next night and cost the girl her

_____. On the third night, she had nothing to offer. "In
　　　NOUN

that case," he said, "your firstborn _____ will be mine." She
　　　　　　　　　　　　　　　　NOUN

_____ agreed. But when the girl was happily married to the
　　ADVERB

king and they had a baby, the little man reappeared. He said, "If you

can guess my name, I will release you from your _____
　　　　　　　　　　　　　　　　　　　　　　　ADJECTIVE

promise." "Rumpelstiltskin," the queen guessed. The little man couldn't

believe his _____. She was right! So Rumpelstiltskin
　　　　PART OF THE BODY (PLURAL)

raced out of the castle in a/an _____ rage.
　　　　　　　　　　　　　　ADJECTIVE

From HAPPILY EVER MAD LIBS® • Copyright © 2010 by Penguin Random House LLC.

HOW TO BE A PRINCESS

PART OF THE BODY —————————————————

ADJECTIVE —————————————————

ADJECTIVE —————————————————

PLURAL NOUN —————————————————

ADJECTIVE —————————————————

ADJECTIVE —————————————————

NOUN —————————————————

ADVERB —————————————————

ADJECTIVE —————————————————

ADJECTIVE —————————————————

ADJECTIVE —————————————————

VERB ENDING IN "ING" —————————————————

ADJECTIVE —————————————————

ADJECTIVE —————————————————

NOUN —————————————————

ADVERB —————————————————

MAD LIBS® is fun to play with friends, but you can also play it by yourself! To begin with, DO NOT look at the story on the page below. Fill in the blanks on this page with the words called for. Then, using the words you have selected, fill in the blank spaces in the story.

Now you've created your own hilarious MAD LIBS® game!

HOW TO BE A PRINCESS

It is difficult not to envy a young woman who has everything her

_____ desires. But history shows it isn't easy being a

PART OF THE BODY

princess. You have to maintain _____ standards and abide

ADJECTIVE

by _____ rules. For example:

ADJECTIVE

- A princess should always be kind to, and understanding of,

  her royal _____. A princess knows that a/an

PLURAL NOUN

  _____ smile is preferable to a/an _____ frown.

ADJECTIVE   ADJECTIVE

- A princess should be a patron of the arts, well-versed in classical

  _____, and _____ familiar with

NOUN   ADVERB

  _____ authors and their _____ works.

ADJECTIVE   ADJECTIVE

- A princess should never make a/an _____ decision. She

                                  ADJECTIVE

  should always think before _____. And when she

VERB ENDING IN "ING"

  does speak, she should be articulate and, if possible, very

  _____.

ADJECTIVE

- And, of course, a princess must be prepared to marry a/an

  _____ _____ and live _____ ever after.

ADJECTIVE   NOUN   ADVERB

From HAPPILY EVER MAD LIBS® • Copyright © 2010 by Penguin Random House LLC.

MAGICAL WEDDING INVITATION

PERSON IN ROOM ———————————

PERSON IN ROOM ———————————

ADJECTIVE ———————————

ADJECTIVE ———————————

CELEBRITY ———————————

PLURAL NOUN ———————————

CELEBRITY ———————————

A PLACE ———————————

ADJECTIVE ———————————

ARTICLE OF CLOTHING (PLURAL) ———————————

NOUN ———————————

PLURAL NOUN ———————————

ADJECTIVE ———————————

PERSON IN ROOM ———————————

PLURAL NOUN ———————————

ADJECTIVE ———————————

MAD LIBS® is fun to play with friends, but you can also play it by yourself! To begin with, DO NOT look at the story on the page below. Fill in the blanks on this page with the words called for. Then, using the words you have selected, fill in the blank spaces in the story.

Now you've created your own hilarious MAD LIBS® game!

MAGICAL WEDDING
INVITATION

You are hereby cordially invited by Queen _____

_____ PERSON IN ROOM

and King _____ to a most _____ event—

_____ PERSON IN ROOM _____ ADJECTIVE

the marriage of Sleeping Beauty to the most _____ Prince

_____ ADJECTIVE

Charming. The bride will be attended by her maid of honor,

_____, and her seven _____, while

CELEBRITY PLURAL NOUN

_____ is the best man. The ceremony will take place in the

CELEBRITY

enchanted forest near (the) _____. All guests are encouraged

A PLACE

to wear _____ dresses or fancy _____.

ADJECTIVE ARTICLE OF CLOTHING (PLURAL)

The dinner menu will include roast _____ and sweet

NOUN

_____ for dessert. The band, _____

PLURAL NOUN ADJECTIVE

_____ and the _____, will provide music

PERSON IN ROOM PLURAL NOUN

for dancing. Please RSVP at your earliest convenience. A/An

_____ time is guaranteed for all.

ADJECTIVE

From HAPPILY EVER MAD LIBS® • Copyright © 2010 by Penguin Random House LLC.

MAD LIBS® is fun to play with friends, but you can also play it by yourself! To begin with, DO NOT look at the story on the page below. Fill in the blanks on this page with the words called for. Then, using the words you have selected, fill in the blank spaces in the story.

Now you've created your own hilarious MAD LIBS® game!

SNOW WHITE AT THE SEVEN DWARFS' COTTAGE

ADJECTIVE _____

PERSON IN ROOM _____

A PLACE _____

ADJECTIVE _____

PLURAL NOUN _____

PLURAL NOUN _____

ADJECTIVE _____

PLURAL NOUN _____

PLURAL NOUN _____

NOUN _____

PERSON IN ROOM _____

PERSON IN ROOM _____

ADJECTIVE _____

ADJECTIVE _____

A PLACE _____

OCCUPATION _____

SNOW WHITE AT THE
SEVEN DWARFS' COTTAGE

My name is Snow White, and I am hiding from my _____

<u>ADJECTIVE</u>

stepmother, _____ , at the Seven Dwarfs' cottage

<u>PERSON IN ROOM</u>

in (the) _____ . It is a/an _____ little place with a

<u>A PLACE</u>   <u>ADJECTIVE</u>

roof made of _____ . Since the dwarfs are letting me stay

<u>PLURAL NOUN</u>

here, I help out by dusting the _____ , cooking

<u>PLURAL NOUN</u>

_____ dinners, and washing their _____ . The

<u>ADJECTIVE</u>   <u>PLURAL NOUN</u>

dwarfs and I have become really close _____ and enjoy one

<u>PLURAL NOUN</u>

another's _____ very much. Their names are Sleepy, Happy,

<u>NOUN</u>

_____ , _____ , Sneezy, _____ ,

<u>PERSON IN ROOM</u>   <u>PERSON IN ROOM</u>   <u>ADJECTIVE</u>

and Doc. The dwarfs and I share many _____ interests. We

<u>ADJECTIVE</u>

especially like to sing, "Hi ho, hi ho, it's off to (the) _____

<u>A PLACE</u>

we go!" Oh, sorry, have to run now. There's a sweet, old _____

<u>OCCUPATION</u>

at the door selling apples.

From HAPPILY EVER MAD LIBS® • Copyright © 2010 by Penguin Random House LLC.

THE GINGERBREAD MAN'S EXERCISE ROUTINE

VERB _____

SAME VERB _____

NOUN _____

ADJECTIVE _____

PLURAL NOUN _____

ADJECTIVE _____

ADVERB _____

ADJECTIVE _____

NOUN _____

PART OF THE BODY (PLURAL) _____

NUMBER _____

NOUN _____

PART OF THE BODY _____

VERB _____

PART OF THE BODY _____

NOUN _____

ADJECTIVE _____

NOUN _____

PLURAL NOUN _____

MAD LIBS® is fun to play with friends, but you can also play it by yourself! To begin with, DO NOT look at the story on the page below. Fill in the blanks on this page with the words called for. Then, using the words you have selected, fill in the blank spaces in the story.

Now you've created your own hilarious MAD LIBS® game!

Christmas Cheer MAD LIBS

THE GINGERBREAD MAN'S EXERCISE ROUTINE

_____, _____ as fast as you can. You can't catch
   VERB   SAME VERB

me—I'm the Gingerbread _____! And I'm known for
                        NOUN

running at _____ speeds to keep people and
         ADJECTIVE

_____ from trying to eat me. I guess it's because I smell
PLURAL NOUN

so _____. But I have to work _____ hard to stay
  ADJECTIVE   ADVERB

in _____ shape. I start my day when the
    ADJECTIVE

_____ comes up. I warm up by stretching to loosen my
 NOUN

_____ for approximately _____
PART OF THE BODY (PLURAL)   NUMBER

minutes. For weight-lifting exercises, I lift a candy _____
                                      NOUN

over my head to strengthen my abs and _____. I do
                             PART OF THE BODY

_____-ups to develop strength in my _____.
  VERB   PART OF THE BODY

And I always eat a healthy breakfast that includes lots of shredded

_____. This routine may sound a little _____,
 NOUN   ADJECTIVE

but it can really make you feel as fit as a/an _____. And
                                    NOUN

you'll never have to worry about getting eaten by hungry

_____!
PLURAL NOUN

From HAPPILY EVER MAD LIBS® • Copyright © 2010 by Penguin Random House LLC.

UNDER THE SEA WITH THE LITTLE MERMAID

_____ PLURAL NOUN

_____ ADJECTIVE

_____ ADJECTIVE

_____ PLURAL NOUN

_____ PERSON IN ROOM

_____ NOUN

_____ PLURAL NOUN

_____ NOUN

_____ PLURAL NOUN

_____ VERB

PART OF THE BODY (PLURAL) _____

_____ VERB

_____ PLURAL NOUN

_____ ADJECTIVE

PART OF THE BODY (PLURAL) _____

_____ PLURAL NOUN

_____ OCCUPATION

_____ ADVERB

_____ NOUN

MAD LIBS® is fun to play with friends, but you can also play it by yourself! To begin with, DO NOT look at the story on the page below. Fill in the blanks on this page with the words called for. Then, using the words you have selected, fill in the blank spaces in the story.

Now you've created your own hilarious MAD LIBS® game!

UNDER THE SEA WITH
THE LITTLE MERMAID

Life under the sea is full of wonder and _____ —especially
_{PLURAL NOUN}

when you're a mermaid and a/an _____ underwater princess
_{ADJECTIVE}

like me! I live on the ocean floor in a/an _____ castle made
_{ADJECTIVE}

of coral _____ . My dad is King _____ ,
_{PLURAL NOUN}   _{PERSON IN ROOM}

ruler of the entire _____ . My friends are fish, dolphins,
_{NOUN}

and underwater _____ . We spend our days exploring
_{PLURAL NOUN}

_____ reefs and searching for sunken _____ .
_{NOUN}   _{PLURAL NOUN}

Sometimes I wonder what it would be like to _____ on land.
_{VERB}

I've heard that people there have _____ instead of
_{PART OF THE BODY (PLURAL)}

fins. And that they _____ around from place to place in
_{VERB}

motorized _____ and wear _____ _____
_{PLURAL NOUN}   _{ADJECTIVE}   _{PLURAL NOUN}

on their _____ . Someday I hope to visit this place
_{PART OF THE BODY (PLURAL)}

so I can meet a handsome _____ and fall _____
_{OCCUPATION}   _{ADVERB}

in love. That would be a mermaid's _____ come true!
_{NOUN}

From HAPPILY EVER MAD LIBS® • Copyright © 2010 by Penguin Random House LLC.

MAD LIBS® is fun to play with friends, but you can also play it by yourself! To begin with, DO NOT look at the story on the page below. Fill in the blanks on this page with the words called for. Then, using the words you have selected, fill in the blank spaces in the story.

Now you've created your own hilarious MAD LIBS® game!

RAPUNZEL'S HAIR TIPS

ADJECTIVE _____

NOUN _____

PLURAL NOUN _____

PLURAL NOUN _____

NOUN _____

NUMBER _____

PLURAL NOUN _____

ADJECTIVE _____

ADJECTIVE _____

NOUN _____

NUMBER _____

PART OF THE BODY _____

ADJECTIVE _____

PERSON IN ROOM _____

ADJECTIVE _____

RAPUNZEL'S HAIR TIPS

Hi, my dears. Rapunzel here. As you may know, I'm famous for my

long and _____ hair. How do I maintain it? Here are some
 <u>ADJECTIVE</u>

tips that will help you get a beautiful _____ just like mine:
 <u>NOUN</u>

• Use shampoo made from all-natural _____ and
 <u>PLURAL NOUN</u>

  _____ .
  <u>PLURAL NOUN</u>

• Be sure to groom your hair with a fine-tooth _____ for
 <u>NOUN</u>

  _____ hours a day.
  <u>NUMBER</u>

• Eat plenty of fresh _____: The natural oils will give your
 <u>PLURAL NOUN</u>

  hair a/an _____ sheen and _____ body.
  <u>ADJECTIVE</u>   <u>ADJECTIVE</u>

• Wash your _____ no more than _____ times
 <u>NOUN</u>   <u>NUMBER</u>

  a day. Otherwise, it will get dry and you may look like you stuck

  your _____ in a light socket.
  <u>PART OF THE BODY</u>

Follow these _____ tips and Prince _____
 <u>ADJECTIVE</u>   <u>PERSON IN ROOM</u>

will be able to climb up your hair and rescue you if you should happen

to be imprisoned in a/an _____ tower!
 <u>ADJECTIVE</u>

From HAPPILY EVER MAD LIBS® • Copyright © 2010 by Penguin Random House LLC.

MAD LIBS® is fun to play with friends, but you can also play it by yourself! To begin with, DO NOT look at the story on the page below. Fill in the blanks on this page with the words called for. Then, using the words you have selected, fill in the blank spaces in the story.

Now you've created your own hilarious MAD LIBS® game!

A NEW FAIRY TALE

ADJECTIVE _____

PERSON IN ROOM _____

NOUN _____

A PLACE _____

ADJECTIVE _____

PART OF THE BODY _____

ADJECTIVE _____

ADJECTIVE _____

ADJECTIVE _____

NOUN _____

NOUN _____

NOUN _____

VERB _____

PLURAL NOUN _____

NOUN _____

ADJECTIVE _____

A NEW FAIRY TALE

Once upon a time, there lived a/an _____, young girl
ADJECTIVE

named _____ who lived in a little wooden
PERSON IN ROOM

_____ by (the) _____. She was a/an
NOUN   A PLACE

_____ child, always willing to lend a/an _____
ADJECTIVE   PART OF THE BODY

to the _____ villagers. She was small and _____
ADJECTIVE   ADJECTIVE

but worked very hard. Then, one day, she happened upon a/an

_____ frog. To her surprise, this little slimy _____
ADJECTIVE   NOUN

could talk! In a deep, croaky voice it said, "I will grant you three wishes,

but then you must give me a/an _____ on the lips." She
NOUN

agreed. And for her first wish, she asked for a new _____ for
NOUN

her parents to live in. For her second, she wished to be able to

_____ like a bird. For her final wish, she asked for all the
VERB

_____ in the world! And it all came to pass just as the frog
PLURAL NOUN

said. The girl kissed the frog and he suddenly turned into a handsome,

young _____. She couldn't believe her _____
NOUN   ADJECTIVE

luck!

From HAPPILY EVER MAD LIBS® • Copyright © 2010 by Penguin Random House LLC.

MAD LIBS® is fun to play with friends, but you can also play it by yourself! To begin with, DO NOT look at the story on the page below. Fill in the blanks on this page with the words called for. Then, using the words you have selected, fill in the blank spaces in the story.

Now you've created your own hilarious MAD LIBS® game!

PINOCCHIO'S DIARY

NOUN _____

ADJECTIVE _____

NOUN _____

ADJECTIVE _____

NOUN _____

NOUN _____

PERSON IN ROOM _____

ADJECTIVE _____

ADJECTIVE _____

ADVERB _____

NOUN _____

PART OF THE BODY (PLURAL) _____

PART OF THE BODY _____

NUMBER _____

NOUN _____

Christmas Cheer MAD LIBS

PINOCCHIO'S DIARY

6:20 a.m.: Woke up this morning, looked at my face in the

_____ , and I was still nothing but a/an _____
  NOUN   ADJECTIVE

puppet carved out of _____ . Depressed, went back to sleep.
                          NOUN

6:50 a.m.: Awakened by a/an _____ fairy. She said that if I
                                 ADJECTIVE

want to become a real _____ , I must have a conscience.
                           NOUN

Then she disappeared into thin _____ .
                                    NOUN

7:12 a.m.: A cricket named _____ visited me. The
                              PERSON IN ROOM

cricket said that a boy with a good conscience can tell right from

_____ , and he always speaks the _____ truth.
   ADJECTIVE   ADJECTIVE

The cricket added that if I lie, it will become _____ apparent
                                                     ADVERB

to everyone.

7:30 a.m.: Excited, I woke up my dad, Geppetto, and told him that I

had become a real _____ , just like he always wanted.
                       NOUN

Geppetto's _____ filled with tears.
              PART OF THE BODY (PLURAL)

8:30 a.m.: Geppetto asked if I would like to go to school. I said yes.

Suddenly my _____ grew _____ inches. I took a
                PART OF THE BODY   NUMBER

solemn _____ never to lie again.
            NOUN

From HAPPILY EVER MAD LIBS® • Copyright © 2010 by Penguin Random House LLC.

MAD LIBS® is fun to play with friends, but you can also play it by yourself! To begin with, DO NOT look at the story on the page below. Fill in the blanks on this page with the words called for. Then, using the words you have selected, fill in the blank spaces in the story.

Now you've created your own hilarious MAD LIBS® game!

MAGIC WAND FOR SALE

OCCUPATION _____

NOUN _____

PLURAL NOUN _____

PLURAL NOUN _____

PLURAL NOUN _____

PERSON IN ROOM _____

PLURAL NOUN _____

PLURAL NOUN _____

ADJECTIVE _____

NUMBER _____

PLURAL NOUN _____

ADJECTIVE _____

ADJECTIVE _____

PLURAL NOUN _____

MAGIC WAND FOR SALE

Are you a wizard, a fairy godmother, or a/an _____ looking
OCCUPATION

for a magic _____ that can do it all? Do you need to turn
NOUN

frogs into _____ or make _____ fly or have an
PLURAL NOUN _PLURAL NOUN_

evil witch vanish into a puff of smoke? Well, look no further! This is

the wand that can do anything! That's right—the Wandinator 2000 is

here! Handcrafted from the finest _____ , this is the same
PLURAL NOUN

wand that the famous wizard _____ uses. With the
PERSON IN ROOM

Wandinator 2000, you, too, can change a pile of worthless

_____ into valuable _____ . Tired of wands
PLURAL NOUN _PLURAL NOUN_

that are _____ and wear out too fast? The Wandinator 2000 is
ADJECTIVE

guaranteed to last _____ years or your _____
NUMBER _PLURAL NOUN_

back! Act now and get a free _____ carrying case. Don't miss
ADJECTIVE

this _____ opportunity. Buy it now! Gold, silver,
ADJECTIVE

_____ , and credit cards accepted.
PLURAL NOUN

From HAPPILY EVER MAD LIBS® • Copyright © 2010 by Penguin Random House LLC.

SO YOU WANT
TO BE A VILLAIN?

ADJECTIVE _____

NOUN _____

PLURAL NOUN _____

ADJECTIVE _____

PERSON IN ROOM _____

PERSON IN ROOM _____

NOUN _____

ADJECTIVE _____

PLURAL NOUN _____

PERSON IN ROOM _____

CELEBRITY _____

PLURAL NOUN _____

OCCUPATION (PLURAL) _____

ADJECTIVE _____

ADJECTIVE _____

ADJECTIVE _____

MAD LIBS® is fun to play with friends, but you can also play it by yourself! To begin with, DO NOT look at the story on the page below. Fill in the blanks on this page with the words called for. Then, using the words you have selected, fill in the blank spaces in the story.

Now you've created your own hilarious MAD LIBS® game!

SO YOU WANT
TO BE A VILLAIN?

It is not easy being a/an _____ villain in a sea of fairy
                              ADJECTIVE

_____-mothers, magical _____, and
        NOUN   PLURAL NOUN

_____ princes and princesses. To be a really successful villain
   ADJECTIVE

like Count _____ or _____ the Wicked
            PERSON IN ROOM   PERSON IN ROOM

_____ will take practice and the right tools. First, you'll
      NOUN

need a really _____ laugh, since you have to cackle alongside
                 ADJECTIVE

the most evil witches and horrible _____. It is also
                                         PLURAL NOUN

recommended that you hire some evil henchmen like

_____ or _____ to help you steal golden
   PERSON IN ROOM   CELEBRITY

_____ or kidnap wealthy _____. And, of
    PLURAL NOUN   OCCUPATION (PLURAL)

course, you'll need a place to hide out. A dark, _____ cave is
                                                      ADJECTIVE

good, but so are _____ alleys. Follow these directions and
                     ADJECTIVE

you will certainly become a really _____, world-famous
                                         ADJECTIVE

villain!

From HAPPILY EVER MAD LIBS® • Copyright © 2010 by Penguin Random House LLC.

MAD LIBS® is fun to play with friends, but you can also play it by yourself! To begin with, DO NOT look at the story on the page below. Fill in the blanks on this page with the words called for. Then, using the words you have selected, fill in the blank spaces in the story.

Now you've created your own hilarious MAD LIBS® game!

THE PRINCESS
AND THE PEA

PERSON IN ROOM _____

PERSON IN ROOM _____

ADJECTIVE _____

ADJECTIVE _____

NOUN _____

NOUN _____

NOUN _____

ADJECTIVE _____

NOUN _____

ADJECTIVE _____

ADJECTIVE _____

ADVERB _____

A PLACE _____

THE PRINCESS
AND THE PEA

There once was a prince named _____. His mother,
<u>PERSON IN ROOM</u>

Queen _____, summoned many princesses to
<u>PERSON IN ROOM</u>

meet him. But none were _____ enough. Then one night,
<u>ADJECTIVE</u>

during a/an _____ storm, the prince heard a loud knock at
<u>ADJECTIVE</u>

the _____. He opened it, and there stood a fair maiden,
<u>NOUN</u>

soaking wet but as beautiful as a summer's _____. It was
<u>NOUN</u>

love at first _____. The girl said she was a princess, but the
<u>NOUN</u>

queen was doubtful. Luckily, she had a way to make sure. She took the

girl to a/an _____ bedroom where she had piled mattress
<u>ADJECTIVE</u>

upon mattress until they almost reached the ceiling. Underneath, she

placed a tiny _____. If the young woman felt the pea
<u>NOUN</u>

through the mattresses, she was really a/an _____ princess.
<u>ADJECTIVE</u>

Sure enough, the next morning, the maiden complained that she was

unable to sleep because the _____ bed was so uncomfortable.
<u>ADJECTIVE</u>

The prince married her and they lived _____ ever after in
<u>ADVERB</u>

(the) _____.
<u>A PLACE</u>

From HAPPILY EVER MAD LIBS® • Copyright © 2010 by Penguin Random House LLC.

MAD LIBS®

WINTER GAMES
MAD LIBS

by Roger Price & Leonard Stern

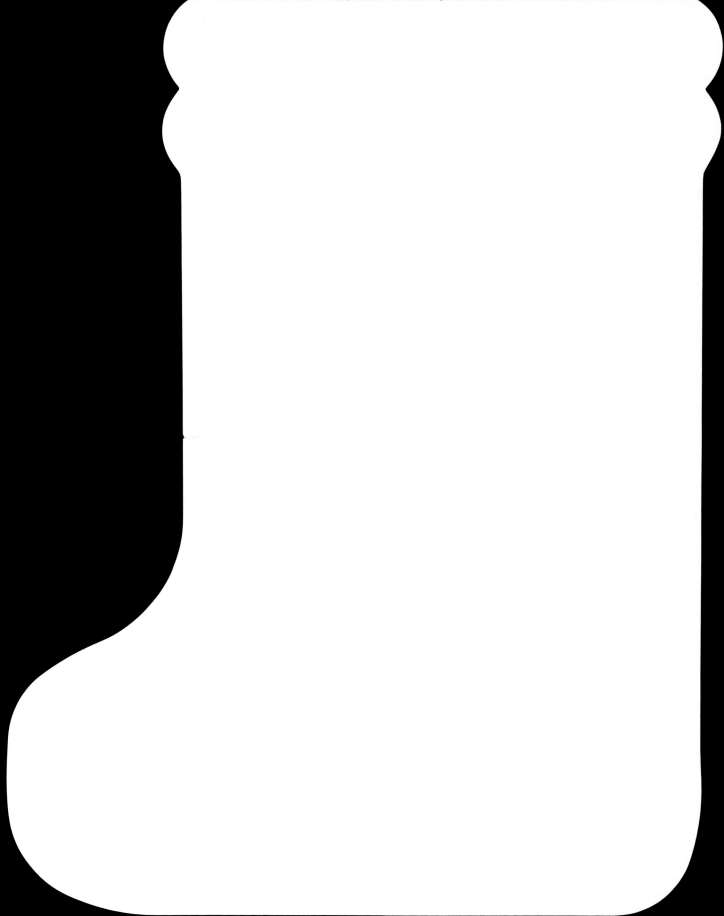

INSTRUCTIONS

MAD LIBS® is a game for people who don't like games! It can be played by one, two, three, four, or forty.

● RIDICULOUSLY SIMPLE DIRECTIONS

In this tablet you will find stories containing blank spaces where words are left out. One player, the READER, selects one of these stories. The READER does not tell anyone what the story is about. Instead, he/she asks the other players, the WRITERS, to give him/her words. These words are used to fill in the blank spaces in the story.

● TO PLAY

The READER asks each WRITER in turn to call out a word—an adjective or a noun or whatever the space calls for—and uses them to fill in the blank spaces in the story. The result is a MAD LIBS® game.

When the READER then reads the completed MAD LIBS® game to the other players, they will discover that they have written a story that is fantastic, screamingly funny, shocking, silly, crazy, or just plain dumb—depending upon which words each WRITER called out.

● EXAMPLE (*Before* and *After*)

"_____!" he said _____
      EXCLAMATION   ADVERB

as he jumped into his convertible _____ and
                                         NOUN

drove off with his _____ wife.
                          ADJECTIVE

"_____OUCH_____!" he said _____STUPIDLY_____
      EXCLAMATION   ADVERB

as he jumped into his convertible _____CAT_____ and
                                         NOUN

drove off with his _____BRAVE_____ wife.
                          ADJECTIVE

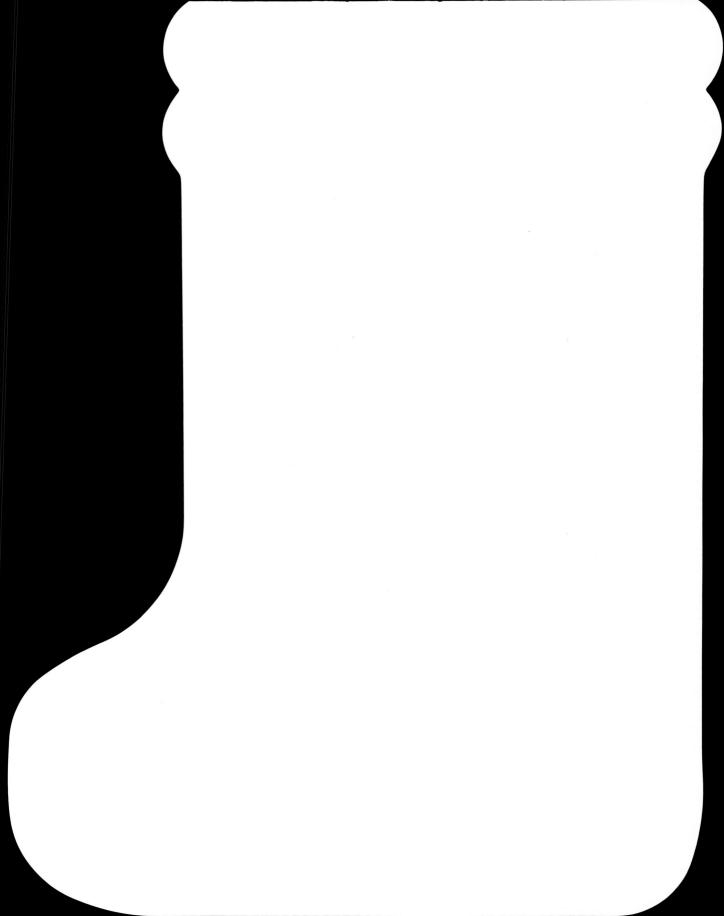

QUICK REVIEW

In case you have forgotten what adjectives, adverbs, nouns, and verbs are, here is a quick review:

An ADJECTIVE describes something or somebody. *Lumpy, soft, ugly, messy,* and *short* are adjectives.

An ADVERB tells how something is done. It modifies a verb and usually ends in "ly." *Modestly, stupidly, greedily,* and *carefully* are adverbs.

A NOUN is the name of a person, place, or thing. *Sidewalk, umbrella, bridle, bathtub,* and *nose* are nouns.

A VERB is an action word. *Run, pitch, jump,* and *swim* are verbs. Put the verbs in past tense if the directions say PAST TENSE. *Ran, pitched, jumped,* and *swam* are verbs in the past tense.

When we ask for A PLACE, we mean any sort of place: a country or city (*Spain, Cleveland*) or a room (*bathroom, kitchen*).

An EXCLAMATION or SILLY WORD is any sort of funny sound, gasp, grunt, or outcry, like *Wow!, Ouch!, Whomp!, Ick!,* and *Gadzooks!*

When we ask for specific words, like a NUMBER, a COLOR, an ANIMAL, or a PART OF THE BODY, we mean a word that is one of those things, like *seven, blue, horse,* or *head.*

When we ask for a PLURAL, it means more than one. For example, *cat* pluralized is *cats.*

DOWNHILL SKI RACE

PLURAL NOUN ——————————————

VERB ——————————————

NOUN ——————————————

ADJECTIVE ——————————————

VERB ENDING IN "ING" ——————————————

NOUN ——————————————

PLURAL NOUN ——————————————

NOUN ——————————————

PART OF THE BODY ——————————————

PLURAL NOUN ——————————————

ADJECTIVE ——————————————

PLURAL NOUN ——————————————

NOUN ——————————————

NOUN ——————————————

PLURAL NOUN ——————————————

MAD LIBS® is fun to play with friends, but you can also play it by yourself! To begin with, DO NOT look at the story on the page below. Fill in the blanks on this page with the words called for. Then, using the words you have selected, fill in the blank spaces in the story.

Now you've created your own hilarious MAD LIBS® game!

DOWNHILL SKI RACE

From the moment the downhill _____ leave the gates until
                              PLURAL NOUN

the second they _____ across the finish line, the ski race is
                    VERB

a/an _____ -pounding experience! The skiers must navigate
        NOUN

a/an _____ demanding course: from _____
        ADJECTIVE   VERB ENDING IN "ING"

over giant mounds of _____ known as "moguls" to
                           NOUN

maneuvering around plastic _____ planted in the snow to
                              PLURAL NOUN

create a more challenging _____. If that isn't tough enough,
                               NOUN

the racers have to combat the elements—the _____ -chilling
                                          PART OF THE BODY

cold, the blinding snow _____, and the _____
                          PLURAL NOUN   ADJECTIVE

winds racing up to 100 _____ per hour. Only the results of
                          PLURAL NOUN

a downhill _____ are predictable. It seems that year after
              NOUN

year, the same team wins this _____. Must be something in
                                   NOUN

their _____ !
       PLURAL NOUN

From WINTER GAMES MAD LIBS® • Copyright © 2005 by Penguin Random House LLC.

TRAITS OF ATHLETES

ADJECTIVE _____

PLURAL NOUN _____

ADJECTIVE _____

NOUN _____

NOUN _____

PLURAL NOUN _____

ADJECTIVE _____

PLURAL NOUN _____

PLURAL NOUN _____

PLURAL NOUN _____

NOUN _____

ADJECTIVE _____

ADJECTIVE _____

NOUN _____

NOUN _____

PLURAL NOUN _____

MAD LIBS® is fun to play with friends, but you can also play it by yourself! To begin with, DO NOT look at the story on the page below. Fill in the blanks on this page with the words called for. Then, using the words you have selected, fill in the blank spaces in the story.

Now you've created your own hilarious MAD LIBS® game!

TRAITS OF ATHLETES

A/An _____ survey of both men and _____
      ADJECTIVE   PLURAL NOUN

winter game athletes reveals some very _____ statistics:
                                          ADJECTIVE

1. 43 percent are ambidextrous. The right _____ always
                                       NOUN

   knows what the left _____ is doing.
                    NOUN

2. 93 percent set impossible _____ for themselves and
                           PLURAL NOUN

   then achieve these _____ goals.
                    ADJECTIVE

3. 47 percent count their calories and eat well-balanced

   _____—observing the recommended allowance of
     PLURAL NOUN

   fruit and _____.
             PLURAL NOUN

4. Slightly over 50 percent play musical _____, the most
                                   PLURAL NOUN

   popular being the piano, violin, and percussion _____.
                                            NOUN

5. 73 percent have a/an _____ sense of timing and
                          ADJECTIVE

   _____ eye-to-_____ coordination.
    ADJECTIVE   NOUN

6. 94 percent never drink hard _____ or smoke
                                NOUN

_____.
   PLURAL NOUN

From WINTER GAMES MAD LIBS® • Copyright © 2005 by Penguin Random House LLC.

FIGURE SKATING

PLURAL NOUN _____

ADVERB _____

PERSON IN ROOM _____

NOUN _____

NOUN _____

ADJECTIVE _____

ADJECTIVE _____

ADJECTIVE _____

NOUN _____

VERB _____

ADJECTIVE _____

NOUN _____

NOUN _____

NOUN _____

ADJECTIVE _____

NOUN _____

PLURAL NOUN _____

NOUN _____

MAD LIBS® is fun to play with friends, but you can also play it by yourself! To begin with, DO NOT look at the story on the page below. Fill in the blanks on this page with the words called for. Then, using the words you have selected, fill in the blank spaces in the story.

Now you've created your own hilarious MAD LIBS® game!

FIGURE SKATING

As a crowd of more than 19,000 _____ filed into the
                                    PLURAL NOUN

_____ designed auditorium, _____,
     ADVERB   PERSON IN ROOM

our _____-skating champion, went through her warm-up
        NOUN

_____. For the first time in her _____ life, the
   NOUN   ADJECTIVE

champion felt frightened and _____. As the music began,
                                 ADJECTIVE

the champion took a/an _____ breath, smoothed the ruffles
                           ADJECTIVE

of her _____, and started to _____. Just as she
         NOUN   VERB

feared, when it came time for her most _____ jump, a triple
                                           ADJECTIVE

_____, she lost her balance and landed with a thump on
   NOUN

her _____. She stood up bravely, brushed the ice off her
        NOUN

_____, and finished her _____ routine. The
   NOUN   ADJECTIVE

crowd gave her a five-minute standing _____. Even though
                                           NOUN

she realized she had lost the competition, she knew she had won the

hearts and _____ of every _____ in the auditorium.
              PLURAL NOUN   NOUN

From WINTER GAMES MAD LIBS® • Copyright © 2005 by Penguin Random House LLC.

RULES FOR A SNOWBALL FIGHT

_____ ADJECTIVE

_____ VERB ENDING IN "ING"

_____ NOUN

_____ PLURAL NOUN

_____ PLURAL NOUN

_____ NOUN

_____ PLURAL NOUN

_____ PART OF THE BODY

_____ NOUN

_____ PLURAL NOUN

_____ PLURAL NOUN

_____ NOUN

_____ ADVERB

_____ ADJECTIVE

_____ NOUN

_____ PLURAL NOUN

_____ ADJECTIVE

_____ NOUN

_____ NOUN

MAD LIBS® is fun to play with friends, but you can also play it by yourself! To begin with, DO NOT look at the story on the page below. Fill in the blanks on this page with the words called for. Then, using the words you have selected, fill in the blank spaces in the story.

Now you've created your own hilarious MAD LIBS® game!

RULES FOR A
SNOWBALL FIGHT

The _____ winter games committee does not recognize
      ADJECTIVE

snowball _____ as an official _____.
     VERB ENDING IN "ING"   NOUN

Nevertheless, it has established rules and _____ for the
                                  PLURAL NOUN

athletes who want to throw icy _____ at each other.
                           PLURAL NOUN

- Contestants can toss only one _____ at a time and from
                                NOUN

  a distance not less than 25 _____ away.
                         PLURAL NOUN

- Aiming at a/an _____ is not permitted. If anybody
               PART OF THE BODY

  is hit below the _____, that person automatically wins.
                NOUN

- Loading a snowball with heavy _____ or solid
                        PLURAL NOUN

  _____ is _____ forbidden. Snowball tampering
    PLURAL NOUN   ADVERB

  will result in _____ penalties or rejection from the
               ADJECTIVE

  _____.
    NOUN

- All _____ must wear _____ gear that protects
     PLURAL NOUN   ADJECTIVE

  their eyes, as well as their _____ and _____.
                   NOUN   NOUN

From WINTER GAMES MAD LIBS® • Copyright © 2005 by Penguin Random House LLC.

MAD LIBS® is fun to play with friends, but you can also play it by yourself! To begin with, DO NOT look at the story on the page below. Fill in the blanks on this page with the words called for. Then, using the words you have selected, fill in the blank spaces in the story.

Now you've created your own hilarious MAD LIBS® game!

A WINTER GAMES BROADCAST

CELEBRITY _____

NOUN _____

NOUN _____

PLURAL NOUN _____

PLURAL NOUN _____

PERSON IN ROOM _____

NOUN _____

NOUN _____

PLURAL NOUN _____

NOUN _____

PLURAL NOUN _____

NOUN _____

ADVERB _____

NOUN _____

PLURAL NOUN _____

SAME PERSON IN ROOM _____

ADJECTIVE _____

A WINTER GAMES
BROADCAST

"Hi, we're broadcasting live from the American compound here at

the ski village. Unfortunately, my co-host, _____, has
                                          CELEBRITY

laryngitis and has lost his _____. He'll be back with us as
                            NOUN

soon as his _____ returns. Now to breaking _____!
            NOUN   PLURAL NOUN

Sadly, we've learned that less than twenty _____ ago,
                                           PLURAL NOUN

_____, America's best _____ skier and
PERSON IN ROOM   NOUN

favorite to win the giant slalom, suffered a life-threatening

_____ when he plummeted 300 _____ down
NOUN   PLURAL NOUN

the side of a/an _____. According to the latest hospital
                 NOUN

_____, he broke his _____, but doctors are
PLURAL NOUN   NOUN

hopeful he'll heal _____ and be back on his _____
                   ADVERB   NOUN

by the end of the year. Our fervent _____ go out to
                                    PLURAL NOUN

_____ and his entire _____ family."
SAME PERSON IN ROOM   ADJECTIVE

From WINTER GAMES MAD LIBS® • Copyright © 2005 by Penguin Random House LLC.

MAD LIBS® is fun to play with friends, but you can also play it by yourself! To begin with, DO NOT look at the story on the page below. Fill in the blanks on this page with the words called for. Then, using the words you have selected, fill in the blank spaces in the story.

Now you've created your own hilarious MAD LIBS® game!

SNOWBOARDING

_____ PLURAL NOUN

_____ NOUN

_____ PLURAL NOUN

_____ PLURAL NOUN

_____ PLURAL NOUN

_____ ADJECTIVE

_____ ADJECTIVE

_____ NOUN

_____ PART OF THE BODY

_____ NOUN

_____ PLURAL NOUN

_____ VERB

_____ NOUN

_____ NOUN

_____ PLURAL NOUN

_____ ADJECTIVE

_____ VERB ENDING IN "ING"

_____ PLURAL NOUN

Christmas Cheer MAD LIBS

SNOWBOARDING

Most of us have watched snowboarding spring up before our very

_____. In its short history, _____-boarding
    PLURAL NOUN   NOUN

has cemented itself into the _____ of sporting
                                PLURAL NOUN

_____ around the world. Its simplicity appeals to men
    PLURAL NOUN

and _____ of all ages. All you need to snowboard is
       PLURAL NOUN

_____ boots, a relatively short _____ board,
    ADJECTIVE   ADJECTIVE

athletic _____, and a willingness to break a/an
             NOUN

_____. I am a high-school _____ who has
  PART OF THE BODY   NOUN

won several _____ in snowboarding competitions. Many
         PLURAL NOUN

of my closest friends say I eat, drink, and _____
                                  VERB

snowboarding. I admit to practicing morning, noon, and

_____, but it paid off last week when I was invited to
    NOUN

qualify for the team in the freestyle _____. This is where I
                              NOUN

can shine. I'm the best at inverted _____, which
                            PLURAL NOUN

are _____ because you're upside down while
      ADJECTIVE

_____. Excuse me, I'm going now. I can't wait to hit
  VERB ENDING IN "ING"

the fresh _____ out on the slopes!
        PLURAL NOUN

From WINTER GAMES MAD LIBS® • Copyright © 2005 by Penguin Random House LLC.

MAD LIBS® is fun to play with friends, but you can also play it by yourself! To begin with, DO NOT look at the story on the page below. Fill in the blanks on this page with the words called for. Then, using the words you have selected, fill in the blank spaces in the story.

Now you've created your own hilarious MAD LIBS® game!

BOBSLEDDING GLOSSARY

_____ PLURAL NOUN

_____ ADJECTIVE

_____ ADJECTIVE

_____ NOUN

_____ PLURAL NOUN

_____ NOUN

_____ NOUN

_____ NOUN

_____ NOUN

_____ PLURAL NOUN

_____ PLURAL NOUN

_____ NOUN

_____ VERB ENDING IN "ING"

_____ ADJECTIVE

_____ VERB

_____ NOUN

_____ PLURAL NOUN

_____ NOUN

BOBSLEDDING GLOSSARY

The name "bobsledding" comes from the early racers bobbing their

_____ back and forth to gain the most _____
PLURAL NOUN   ADJECTIVE

speed. Here are some _____ phrases to provide a better
                          ADJECTIVE

understanding of this high-speed _____.
                                        NOUN

Bobsled: a large sled made up of two _____ linked
                                              PLURAL NOUN

together. There are two sizes, a two-person _____ and a
                                                   NOUN

four- _____ sled.
         NOUN

Brakeman: the last _____ to leap onto the _____.
                            NOUN   NOUN

The brakeman applies the _____ to bring it to a stop and
                              PLURAL NOUN

must have very strong _____.
                           PLURAL NOUN

Driver: the front _____ in the bobsled is responsible for
                           NOUN

_____. The driver's _____ goal is to
VERB ENDING IN "ING"   ADJECTIVE

maintain the straightest path down the track.

Pushtime: the amount of time required to _____ a/an
                                                  VERB

_____ over the first 50 _____ of a run.
     NOUN   PLURAL NOUN

WH: abbreviation for "what happened?" Usually said when the

_____ crashes!
     NOUN

From WINTER GAMES MAD LIBS® • Copyright © 2005 by Penguin Random House LLC.

MAD LIBS® is fun to play with friends, but you can also play it by yourself! To begin with, DO NOT look at the story on the page below. Fill in the blanks on this page with the words called for. Then, using the words you have selected, fill in the blank spaces in the story.

Now you've created your own hilarious MAD LIBS® game!

SNOWMAN-BUILDING

ADJECTIVE _____

NOUN _____

NOUN _____

ADJECTIVE _____

NOUN _____

ADJECTIVE _____

PLURAL NOUN _____

PART OF THE BODY (PLURAL) _____

NOUN _____

COLOR _____

NOUN _____

PLURAL NOUN _____

ADJECTIVE _____

NOUN _____

NOUN _____

ADJECTIVE _____

NOUN _____

NOUN _____

SNOWMAN-BUILDING

Question: What kid hasn't loved the _____ thrill of building
ADJECTIVE

a/an _____ -man?
NOUN

Answer: Kids who live where the _____ never stops shining.
NOUN

Nevertheless, snowman-building is one of the most _____
ADJECTIVE

competitions at the winter games. Each team is given several hundred

pounds of powdered _____ to mold and shape into what
NOUN

they hope will be the most _____ snowman anyone has ever
ADJECTIVE

laid _____ on. This year's winner was so adorable that
PLURAL NOUN

everyone wanted to throw their _____ around him
PART OF THE BODY (PLURAL)

and hug his _____. They used a bright _____
NOUN   COLOR

_____ for his nose, two shiny _____ for his eyes
NOUN   PLURAL NOUN

and a/an _____ _____ on his head for a hat. In
ADJECTIVE   NOUN

addition, they put a corncob _____ in his mouth and tied
NOUN

a/an _____ scarf around his neck. Their prizewinning
ADJECTIVE

_____ quickly became the talk of the _____.
NOUN   NOUN

From WINTER GAMES MAD LIBS® • Copyright © 2005 by Penguin Random House LLC.

FACE-OFF

NOUN _____

NOUN _____

ADJECTIVE _____

NOUN _____

NOUN _____

NOUN _____

ADJECTIVE _____

NOUN _____

ADJECTIVE _____

NOUN _____

NOUN _____

PLURAL NOUN _____

ADVERB _____

PLURAL NOUN _____

PLURAL NOUN _____

ADJECTIVE _____

NOUN _____

PLURAL NOUN _____

MAD LIBS® is fun to play with friends, but you can also play it by yourself. To begin with, DO NOT look at the story on the page below. Fill in the blanks on this page with the words called for. Then, using the words you have selected, fill in the blank spaces in the story.

Now you've created your own hilarious MAD LIBS® game!

FACE-OFF

If you're seeking fame and _____ as a hockey player, you
NOUN

may want to give it a second _____. Hockey is not a sport
NOUN

for the _____ of heart! You put your _____ in
ADJECTIVE   NOUN

danger the moment you enter the rink and skate onto the

_____. Hockey is a game of vicious _____
NOUN   NOUN

contact. To be a/an _____ hockey player you have to keep
ADJECTIVE

your _____ in perfect shape, you have to be lean and
NOUN

_____, and you can't afford one extra ounce of
ADJECTIVE

_____ on your _____. Hockey attracts the most
NOUN   NOUN

volatile _____. These fans can become _____
PLURAL NOUN   ADVERB

physical and throw soda _____, large sticks and
PLURAL NOUN

_____, and even _____ coins onto the ice. You
PLURAL NOUN   ADJECTIVE

can see why hockey is considered the most physical _____
NOUN

of all the _____ at the winter games.
PLURAL NOUN

From WINTER GAMES MAD LIBS® • Copyright © 2005 by Penguin Random House LLC.

DOGS AND SLEDS

PLURAL NOUN _____

PLURAL NOUN _____

NOUN _____

PART OF THE BODY _____

ADVERB _____

NOUN _____

NOUN _____

PLURAL NOUN _____

PLURAL NOUN _____

NUMBER _____

ADJECTIVE _____

PLURAL NOUN _____

NOUN _____

NOUN _____

PLURAL NOUN _____

NOUN _____

NOUN _____

MAD LIBS® is fun to play with friends, but you can also play it by yourself! To begin with, DO NOT look at the story on the page below. Fill in the blanks on this page with the words called for. Then, using the words you have selected, fill in the blank spaces in the story.

Now you've created your own hilarious MAD LIBS® game!

DOGS AND SLEDS

Of all the winter _____, dogsled racing is my favorite.
                        PLURAL NOUN

Watching these beautiful four-legged _____ courageously
                                        PLURAL NOUN

pull the sled across the frozen _____ tugs at my
                                      NOUN

_____-strings. The rules for dogsled racing are
PART OF THE BODY

_____ simple—the first team to cross the finish
        ADVERB

_____ wins the _____. A dogsled team consists
      NOUN   NOUN

of 14 Siberian _____, each weighing approximately 50
                    PLURAL NOUN

_____ and each able to pull _____ times its
  PLURAL NOUN   NUMBER

weight. These beautiful and _____ dogs are trained to
                                ADJECTIVE

respond to the shouted _____ of their _____.
                          PLURAL NOUN   NOUN

The driver stands on a/an _____ at the rear of the sled and
                              NOUN

guides the dogs with verbal _____ and, if necessary, a crack
                                PLURAL NOUN

of the _____. Dogsled races are proof positive why a dog is
          NOUN

thought of as man's best _____.
                              NOUN

From WINTER GAMES MAD LIBS® • Copyright © 2005 by Penguin Random House LLC.

THE LODGE

NOUN _____

NOUN _____

NOUN _____

NOUN _____

PLURAL NOUN _____

NOUN _____

ADJECTIVE _____

NOUN _____

NOUN _____

VERB ENDING IN "ING" _____

PART OF THE BODY _____

NOUN _____

NOUN _____

PLURAL NOUN _____

PLURAL NOUN _____

NOUN _____

ADJECTIVE _____

PLURAL NOUN _____

MAD LIBS® is fun to play with friends, but you can also play it by yourself! To begin with, DO NOT look at the story on the page below. Fill in the blanks on this page with the words called for. Then, using the words you have selected, fill in the blank spaces in the story.

Now you've created your own hilarious MAD LIBS® game!

THE LODGE

A/An _____ away from home is most important to a
         NOUN

competitive _____. Athletes should select a lodge
                 NOUN

recommended by a travel _____, the automobile
                              NOUN

_____, or even relatives or close _____. The bedroom
      NOUN   PLURAL NOUN

should have a king-size _____ with a/an _____
                            NOUN   ADJECTIVE

mattress to ensure a good night's _____. If possible, there
                                       NOUN

should be a hot _____ to relax those aching muscles after a
                     NOUN

long day of _____. Since relaxation is so important to
              VERB ENDING IN "ING"

an athlete's _____, the lodge should also provide an
               PART OF THE BODY

outdoor swimming _____. Other amenities might be a
                      NOUN

wood-burning _____, a game room stocked with arcade
                  NOUN

_____, and game tables for chess or _____, as
  PLURAL NOUN   PLURAL NOUN

well as a Ping-Pong _____. Since nutrition is of
                        NOUN

_____ significance to athletes, the lodge's restaurant should
  ADJECTIVE

have a rating of five _____.
                         PLURAL NOUN

From WINTER GAMES MAD LIBS® • Copyright © 2005 by Penguin Random House LLC.

SAGE ADVICE

VERB ENDING IN "ING" _____

PERSON IN ROOM _____

ADJECTIVE _____

ADJECTIVE _____

PLURAL NOUN _____

ADVERB _____

PLURAL NOUN _____

ADJECTIVE _____

PLURAL NOUN _____

NOUN _____

ADJECTIVE _____

PLURAL NOUN _____

PLURAL NOUN _____

VERB ENDING IN "ING" _____

NOUN _____

MAD LIBS® is fun to play with friends, but you can also play it by yourself! To begin with, DO NOT look at the story on the page below. Fill in the blanks on this page with the words called for. Then, using the words you have selected, fill in the blank spaces in the story.

Now you've created your own hilarious MAD LIBS® game!

SAGE ADVICE

According to the pioneer of downhill _____,
                                        VERB ENDING IN "ING"
_____, "When you ski, your _____ equipment
    PERSON IN ROOM   ADJECTIVE
should be the equal of your _____ ability." Remember this
                                 ADJECTIVE
sage advice when purchasing your first pair of _____. It is
                                                    PLURAL NOUN
_____ important to take many _____ into
    ADVERB   PLURAL NOUN
consideration before plunking down _____ bucks for your
                                          ADJECTIVE
_____. Your gender, your height, and your _____
  PLURAL NOUN   NOUN
are all _____ factors in selecting a pair of _____
            ADJECTIVE   PLURAL NOUN
that match your skills and _____. It goes without
                                PLURAL NOUN
_____: If you don't have the right skis, you're starting
VERB ENDING IN "ING"
off on the wrong _____.
                      NOUN

From WINTER GAMES MAD LIBS® • Copyright © 2005 by Penguin Random House LLC.

MAD LIBS® is fun to play with friends, but you can also play it by yourself! To begin with, DO NOT look at the story on the page below. Fill in the blanks on this page with the words called for. Then, using the words you have selected, fill in the blank spaces in the story.

Now you've created your own hilarious MAD LIBS® game!

MORE SAGE ADVICE

NOUN _____

NOUN _____

PLURAL NOUN _____

ADVERB _____

ADJECTIVE _____

PART OF THE BODY _____

NOUN _____

ADJECTIVE _____

NOUN _____

PART OF THE BODY _____

ADJECTIVE _____

NOUN _____

NOUN _____

ADJECTIVE _____

NOUN _____

NOUN _____

MORE SAGE ADVICE

Beware! If your skiing equipment isn't top-of-the-_____,
                                                    NOUN
you put your _____ at risk. Here are some important
                  NOUN
_____ to remember:
PLURAL NOUN

Ski Boots: Give careful thought to this important piece of
equipment. Choose _____. Together with ski bindings,
                        ADVERB
these _____ boots form the link between your skis and
         ADJECTIVE
your _____.
      PART OF THE BODY

Ski Bindings: As far as your safety is concerned, _____
                                                         NOUN
bindings are the most _____ pieces of _____ in
                          ADJECTIVE   NOUN
skiing.

Ski Helmets: Protect your _____ by wearing a/an
                                PART OF THE BODY
_____ ski _____. Helmets absolutely help you
ADJECTIVE   NOUN
avoid a serious _____ mishap.
                   NOUN

Ski Clothing: First and foremost, get yourself some _____
                                                          ADJECTIVE
underwear, preferably thermal, to keep your _____ warm.
                                               NOUN
You will also need a ski _____ to protect your head and ears
                           NOUN
from extremely frigid temperatures.

From WINTER GAMES MAD LIBS® • Copyright © 2005 by Penguin Random House LLC.

SLED RACE

NOUN _____

NOUN _____

NOUN _____

PLURAL NOUN _____

NOUN _____

PLURAL NOUN _____

PLURAL NOUN _____

NOUN _____

ADJECTIVE _____

PLURAL NOUN _____

ADJECTIVE _____

NOUN _____

ADJECTIVE _____

NOUN _____

PLURAL NOUN _____

PART OF THE BODY _____

ADJECTIVE _____

PLURAL NOUN _____

MAD LIBS® is fun to play with friends, but you can also play it by yourself! To begin with, DO NOT look at the story on the page below. Fill in the blanks on this page with the words called for. Then, using the words you have selected, fill in the blank spaces in the story.

Now you've created your own hilarious MAD LIBS® game!

SLED RACE

Ever since I was in the fifth _____ in school, I've dreamed of
                                            NOUN

having my own sled. I started delivering the morning _____
                                           NOUN

on my two-wheeler _____ until I saved enough pennies,
                       NOUN

nickels, and _____ to buy one. It was the smartest
             PLURAL NOUN

_____ I ever made. Today, I am a champion sled racer with
    NOUN

nine first-place _____, seven second-place _____,
              PLURAL NOUN   PLURAL NOUN

one third-place _____, and four _____ ribbons.
             NOUN   ADJECTIVE

Although some of my competitors use sophisticated and aerodynamic

_____, I still rely on a/an _____ version of my
   PLURAL NOUN   ADJECTIVE

old sledding _____. Sled racing is relatively simple; the
              NOUN

participants line up at the top of a/an _____ hill. When the
                               ADJECTIVE

starter drops his _____, the competitors climb on their
               NOUN

_____ and race at break-_____ speed to cross
  PLURAL NOUN   PART OF THE BODY

the _____ line ahead of the other _____.
    ADJECTIVE   PLURAL NOUN

From WINTER GAMES MAD LIBS® • Copyright © 2005 by Penguin Random House LLC.

SKI JUMPING

NOUN _____

NOUN _____

ADJECTIVE _____

NOUN _____

PLURAL NOUN _____

NOUN _____

ADVERB _____

NOUN _____

ADJECTIVE _____

NOUN _____

NOUN _____

PLURAL NOUN _____

PART OF THE BODY _____

NOUN _____

PART OF THE BODY _____

VERB ENDING IN "ING" _____

PLURAL NOUN _____

PLURAL NOUN _____

MAD LIBS® is fun to play with friends, but you can also play it by yourself! To begin with, DO NOT look at the story on the page below. Fill in the blanks on this page with the words called for. Then, using the words you have selected, fill in the blank spaces in the story.

Now you've created your own hilarious MAD LIBS® game!

Christmas Cheer MAD LIBS

SKI JUMPING

Whether you're a/an _____ seated in the stands or a/an
                        NOUN

_____ watching on television, the _____ beauty
      NOUN   ADJECTIVE

of ski jumping is dramatically apparent. What compares to a skier

taking flight, soaring into the crystal-clear _____, against a
                                                    NOUN

background of blue _____ with _____-capped
                       PLURAL NOUN   NOUN

mountains looming _____ in the distance? But
                        ADVERB

_____ jumping doesn't shortchange you on thrills. There's
      NOUN

_____ drama in every jump. You can't help but sit on the
   ADJECTIVE

edge of your _____ and hold your _____ as
                    NOUN   NOUN

conflicting _____ race through your _____.
                PLURAL NOUN   PART OF THE BODY

Will the skier break the world _____? Will he or she
                                     NOUN

break a/an _____? Minutes later, the crowd is
                PART OF THE BODY

_____ at the top of their _____ and you
 VERB ENDING IN "ING"   PLURAL NOUN

have your answer. You've got a world champion on your

_____.
   PLURAL NOUN

From WINTER GAMES MAD LIBS® • Copyright © 2005 by Penguin Random House LLC.

MAD LIBS® is fun to play with friends, but you can also play it by yourself! To begin with, DO NOT look at the story on the page below. Fill in the blanks on this page with the words called for. Then, using the words you have selected, fill in the blank spaces in the story.

Now you've created your own hilarious MAD LIBS® game!

SPEED SKATING

NOUN _____

ADVERB _____

NOUN _____

PLURAL NOUN _____

PART OF THE BODY (PLURAL) _____

NOUN _____

VERB ENDING IN "ING" _____

NOUN _____

NOUN _____

PLURAL NOUN _____

PLURAL NOUN _____

ADVERB _____

NOUN _____

PART OF THE BODY _____

COLOR _____

SPEED SKATING

A speed-skating _____ goes by so _____ that if you
NOUN   ADVERB

blink a/an _____ , you might miss the race. In every
NOUN

competition, skaters not only race against their fellow

_____ , they also challenge the _____
PLURAL NOUN   PART OF THE BODY (PLURAL)

of the clock. They know a fraction of a/an _____ can be the
NOUN

difference between not only winning but _____ a
VERB ENDING IN "ING"

record. Consequently, skaters worship at the shrine of speed. When

racing, they skate bent over, angled toward the ice, with one

_____ behind them, pressed firmly against their
NOUN

_____ , to eliminate being slowed down by wind resistance.
NOUN

They even wear skintight _____ to improve their speed.
PLURAL NOUN

And, as you can tell from their trim, muscular _____ ,
PLURAL NOUN

skaters are _____ weight-conscious. An extra ounce of
ADVERB

_____ strikes terror in a skater's _____ . To say
NOUN   PART OF THE BODY

speed skating is stressful is like calling a kettle _____ !
COLOR

From WINTER GAMES MAD LIBS® • Copyright © 2005 by Penguin Random House LLC.

MAD LIBS® is fun to play with friends, but you can also play it by yourself! To begin with, DO NOT look at the story on the page below. Fill in the blanks on this page with the words called for. Then, using the words you have selected, fill in the blank spaces in the story.

Now you've created your own hilarious MAD LIBS® game!

THE LUGE

ADJECTIVE _____

PLURAL NOUN _____

PLURAL NOUN _____

NOUN _____

NOUN _____

PLURAL NOUN _____

PLURAL NOUN _____

NOUN _____

PART OF THE BODY (PLURAL) _____

PLURAL NOUN _____

NOUN _____

NOUN _____

PART OF THE BODY (PLURAL) _____

ADJECTIVE _____

PLURAL NOUN _____

ADJECTIVE _____

NOUN _____

Christmas Cheer MAD LIBS

THE LUGE

Although the _____ luge is thought to be relatively new, it's
            ADJECTIVE

actually one of the oldest of all winter _____. It was a
                                          PLURAL NOUN

favorite activity of kings, queens, and _____ in the
                                          PLURAL NOUN

eighteenth century. The word comes from the French _____
                                                      NOUN

for sled. The luge travels at a/an _____-threatening speed,
                                     NOUN

often exceeding 75 _____ per hour. Luge athletes become
                     PLURAL NOUN

virtual flying _____ from the moment they step into the
                PLURAL NOUN

_____, lie flat on their _____, and, with
   NOUN   PART OF THE BODY (PLURAL)

their _____ looking up into the sky, push off. As they fly
        PLURAL NOUN

down the ice-covered _____, they steer the _____
                        NOUN   NOUN

by pressing their _____ against the front runners.
                   PART OF THE BODY (PLURAL)

Protected only by a/an _____ helmet, they risk their
                          ADJECTIVE

_____ and are in _____ danger until they speed
   PLURAL NOUN   ADJECTIVE

across the finish _____!
                     NOUN

From WINTER GAMES MAD LIBS® • Copyright © 2005 by Penguin Random House LLC.

MAD LIBS® is fun to play with friends, but you can also play it by yourself! To begin with, DO NOT look at the story on the page below. Fill in the blanks on this page with the words called for. Then, using the words you have selected, fill in the blank spaces in the story.

Now you've created your own hilarious MAD LIBS® game!

IGLOO-BUILDING CONTEST

ADJECTIVE _____

NOUN _____

PLURAL NOUN _____

ADJECTIVE _____

PLURAL NOUN _____

PLURAL NOUN _____

PLURAL NOUN _____

ADVERB _____

ADJECTIVE _____

PLURAL NOUN _____

NOUN _____

ADVERB _____

NOUN _____

ADJECTIVE _____

ADJECTIVE _____

PLURAL NOUN _____

NOUN _____

ADJECTIVE _____

IGLOO-BUILDING CONTEST

Building an igloo is _____ and fun. A hard field of snow is
                          ADJECTIVE

required to build a/an _____ with a dome. The first rule is
                          NOUN

to pack the frozen _____ into _____ blocks of
                      PLURAL NOUN   ADJECTIVE

all shapes and _____. Large _____ are used as
                  PLURAL NOUN   PLURAL NOUN

the base of the dome and the smaller _____ go on the top.
                                        PLURAL NOUN

Then, each block should be smooth and angled _____ to
                                                  ADVERB

make a/an _____ bond with the other _____.
              ADJECTIVE   PLURAL NOUN

Admittedly, building a/an _____ is _____ more
                              NOUN   ADVERB

difficult than pitching a/an _____, but it keeps the
                                NOUN

_____ air out better than a tent. A well-built, average-size
  ADJECTIVE

igloo can accommodate three adults or five _____
                                              ADJECTIVE

_____. Believe it or not, _____-building
  PLURAL NOUN   NOUN

contests are now being held all over—wherever the climate is

_____.
  ADJECTIVE

From WINTER GAMES MAD LIBS® • Copyright © 2005 by Penguin Random House LLC.

MAD LIBS® is fun to play with friends, but you can also play it by yourself! To begin with, DO NOT look at the story on the page below. Fill in the blanks on this page with the words called for. Then, using the words you have selected, fill in the blank spaces in the story.

Now you've created your own hilarious MAD LIBS® game!

SKIING DISCIPLINES

PLURAL NOUN _____

ADJECTIVE _____

NOUN _____

PLURAL NOUN _____

ADJECTIVE _____

VERB ENDING IN "ING" _____

PLURAL NOUN _____

ADJECTIVE _____

PLURAL NOUN _____

PLURAL NOUN _____

ADJECTIVE _____

ADJECTIVE _____

PLURAL NOUN _____

SKIING DISCIPLINES

Skiing comes in different _____, and each has its own

PLURAL NOUN

_____ features offering a different kind of excitement and

ADJECTIVE

_____ for skiers of all _____.

NOUN _PLURAL NOUN_

Alpine Skiing: This _____ form of skiing is the most general

ADJECTIVE

_____ discipline and is practiced equally by men and

VERB ENDING IN "ING"

_____.

PLURAL NOUN

Telemark Skiing: This is a/an _____ style of skiing. It uses

ADJECTIVE

a turning technique that is admired by many _____ and

PLURAL NOUN

mastered by few _____.

PLURAL NOUN

Freestyle Skiing: This takes skiing to _____ heights, using

ADJECTIVE

skis in many _____ ways to come up with _____

ADJECTIVE _ADJECTIVE_

new disciplines, jumps, and _____.

PLURAL NOUN

From WINTER GAMES MAD LIBS® • Copyright © 2005 by Penguin Random House LLC.

MAD LIBS® is fun to play with friends, but you can also play it by yourself! To begin with, DO NOT look at the story on the page below. Fill in the blanks on this page with the words called for. Then, using the words you have selected, fill in the blank spaces in the story.

Now you've created your own hilarious MAD LIBS® game!

Q&A WITH A
CHAMPION ICE-FISHER

NOUN _____

NOUN _____

PLURAL NOUN _____

PLURAL NOUN _____

NUMBER _____

NOUN _____

NOUN _____

NOUN _____

NOUN _____

ADJECTIVE _____

PLURAL NOUN _____

NOUN _____

PLURAL NOUN _____

NOUN _____

PLURAL NOUN _____

ADJECTIVE _____

NOUN _____

Q&A WITH A
CHAMPION ICE-FISHER

Q: How does it feel to win a gold _____?
                                        NOUN

A: I'm bursting with _____. It's as if I've won a million _____.
                         NOUN   PLURAL NOUN

Q: How do you always know there are _____ under the ice?
                                        PLURAL NOUN

A: You don't. You may have to drill more than _____ holes
                                                  NUMBER

in the _____ to catch your first _____.
       NOUN   NOUN

Q: What's the most important safety _____ you can give a
                                        NOUN

would-be _____-fisher?
         NOUN

A: I always tell them what my _____ grandfather told me:
                                  ADJECTIVE

Do not drill a fishing hole bigger than your waistline!

Q: When you ice-fish, you're battling the _____. How do
                                              PLURAL NOUN

you protect yourself against the _____-chilling cold?
                                 NOUN

A: You have to wear protective _____ or you'll freeze your
                                   PLURAL NOUN

_____. I suggest heavy boots, wool-lined _____,
NOUN   PLURAL NOUN

and, of course, _____ johns are a must.
                ADJECTIVE

Q: When is it better to just stay in the comfort of your _____?
                                                             NOUN

A: Again, as my grandfather used to say: "If the wind is from the east,

fishing is the least."

From WINTER GAMES MAD LIBS® • Copyright © 2005 by Penguin Random House LLC.

MAD LIBS® is fun to play with friends, but you can also play it by yourself! To begin with, DO NOT look at the story on the page below. Fill in the blanks on this page with the words called for. Then, using the words you have selected, fill in the blank spaces in the story.

Now you've created your own hilarious MAD LIBS® game!

AWARD CEREMONIES

_____ ADJECTIVE

_____ NOUN

_____ PLURAL NOUN

_____ PLURAL NOUN

_____ NOUN

_____ PART OF THE BODY

_____ ADJECTIVE

_____ NOUN

_____ ADJECTIVE

_____ PLURAL NOUN

_____ ADJECTIVE

_____ ADJECTIVE

_____ PLURAL NOUN

_____ PLURAL NOUN

AWARD CEREMONIES

By far, the most touching and _____ moments of the games
                                        ADJECTIVE

are the _____ ceremonies in which first-, second-, and
             NOUN

third-place _____ are presented to the winning
               PLURAL NOUN

_____. There's hardly a dry _____ in the stadium
  PLURAL NOUN   *NOUN*

when the officials shake the athlete's _____ and place
                                PART OF THE BODY

the _____ medal around his/her _____. Perhaps
    ADJECTIVE   *NOUN*

the most memorable and meaningful moment occurs when the

_____ winner is handed a bouquet of _____
    ADJECTIVE   *PLURAL NOUN*

and the _____ anthem of his/her country is played. When
        ADJECTIVE

the song ends, the athletes usually break into _____ smiles,
                                  ADJECTIVE

lift their _____ high in the air, and acknowledge the
      PLURAL NOUN

crowd by waving their _____.
            PLURAL NOUN

From WINTER GAMES MAD LIBS® • Copyright © 2005 by Penguin Random House LLC.

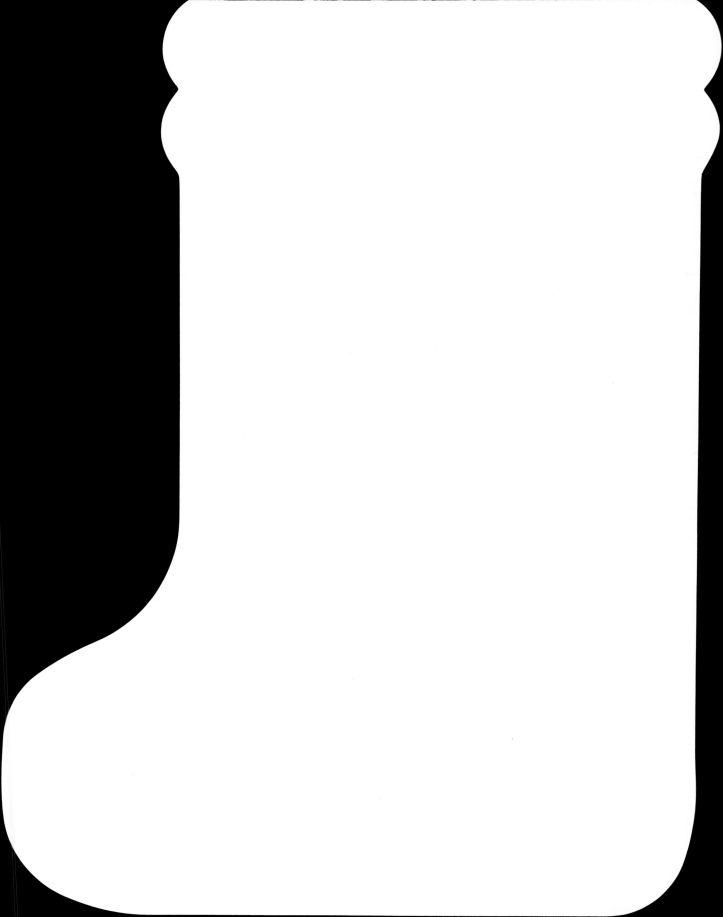

MAD LIBS®
CHRISTMAS FUN
MAD LIBS

by Roger Price & Leonard Stern

INSTRUCTIONS

MAD LIBS® is a game for people who don't like games!
It can be played by one, two, three, four, or forty.

• RIDICULOUSLY SIMPLE DIRECTIONS

In this tablet you will find stories containing blank spaces where words are left out. One player, the READER, selects one of these stories. The READER does not tell anyone what the story is about. Instead, he/she asks the other players, the WRITERS, to give him/her words. These words are used to fill in the blank spaces in the story.

• TO PLAY

The READER asks each WRITER in turn to call out a word—an adjective or a noun or whatever the space calls for—and uses them to fill in the blank spaces in the story. The result is a MAD LIBS® game.

When the READER then reads the completed MAD LIBS® game to the other players, they will discover that they have written a story that is fantastic, screamingly funny, shocking, silly, crazy, or just plain dumb—depending upon which words each WRITER called out.

• EXAMPLE (Before and After)

"_____," he said _____
          EXCLAMATION   ADVERB

as he jumped into his convertible _____ and
                                          NOUN

drove off with his _____ wife.
                        ADJECTIVE

"OU(H!" he said STUPIDLY
   EXCLAMATION   ADVERB

as he jumped into his convertible (AT) and
                                   NOUN

drove off with his BRAVE wife.
                    ADJECTIVE

QUICK REVIEW

In case you have forgotten what adjectives, adverbs, nouns, and verbs are, here is a quick review:

An ADJECTIVE describes something or somebody. *Lumpy, soft, ugly, messy,* and *short* are adjectives.

An ADVERB tells how something is done. It modifies a verb and usually ends in "ly." *Modestly, stupidly, greedily,* and *carefully* are adverbs.

A NOUN is the name of a person, place, or thing. *Sidewalk, umbrella, bridle, bathtub,* and *nose* are nouns.

A VERB is an action word. *Run, pitch, jump,* and *swim* are verbs. Put the verbs in past tense if the directions say PAST TENSE. *Ran, pitched, jumped,* and *swam* are verbs in the past tense.

When we ask for A PLACE, we mean any sort of place: a country or city (*Spain, Cleveland*) or a room (*bathroom, kitchen*).

An EXCLAMATION or SILLY WORD is any sort of funny sound, gasp, grunt, or outcry, like *Wow!, Ouch!, Whomp!, Ick!,* and *Gadzooks!*

When we ask for specific words, like a NUMBER, a COLOR, an ANIMAL, or a PART OF THE BODY, we mean a word that is one of those things, like *seven, blue, horse,* or *head.*

When we ask for a PLURAL, it means more than one. For example, *cat* pluralized is *cats.*

MAD LIBS® is fun to play with friends, but you can also play it by yourself! To begin with, DO NOT look at the story on the page below. Fill in the blanks on this page with the words called for. Then, using the words you have selected, fill in the blank spaces in the story.

Now you've created your own hilarious MAD LIBS® game!

SELECTING A TREE

ADJECTIVE _____

ADJECTIVE _____

NOUN _____

PLURAL NOUN _____

PLURAL NOUN _____

NOUN _____

NOUN _____

NOUN _____

ADJECTIVE _____

NOUN _____

NUMBER _____

PLURAL NOUN _____

NOUN _____

COLOR _____

COLOR _____

NOUN _____

PERSON IN ROOM _____

PERSON IN ROOM _____

Christmas Cheer MAD LIBS

SELECTING A TREE

No Christmas season can be really _____ unless you have
 ADJECTIVE

a/an _____ tree in your _____. If you live in a
 ADJECTIVE NOUN

city, you will see many vacant _____ filled with hundreds
 PLURAL NOUN

of _____ for sale. If you live in the country, you can get
 PLURAL NOUN

your own _____ right out of the forest. Go out with
 NOUN

a/an _____ and _____, and when you see a/an
 NOUN NOUN

_____ tree you like, you can dig it up and plant it in a/an
 ADJECTIVE

_____. Then you can use it for _____ years. To make
 NOUN NUMBER

sure your tree is fresh, shake the branches and see if the _____
 PLURAL NOUN

fall off onto the _____. And make sure the tree is very
 NOUN

_____. Nothing looks worse than a/an _____
 COLOR COLOR

tree. Just follow these directions and you can have a perfectly beautiful

_____ in your front room for weeks. Remember, poems
 NOUN

and Mad Libs are made by fools like _____, but only
 PERSON IN ROOM

_____ can make a tree.
 PERSON IN ROOM

From CHRISTMAS FUN MAD LIBS® • Copyright © 2001, 1985 by Penguin Random House LLC.

MAD LIBS® is fun to play with friends, but you can also play it by yourself! To begin with, DO NOT look at the story on the page below. Fill in the blanks on this page with the words called for. Then, using the words you have selected, fill in the blank spaces in the story.

Now you've created your own hilarious MAD LIBS® game!

DECORATING THE TREE

PERSON IN ROOM ——————————————

VERB ——————————————

PERSON IN ROOM ——————————————

PLURAL NOUN ——————————————

PERSON IN ROOM ——————————————

TYPE OF FOOD (PLURAL) ——————————————

TYPE OF FOOD (PLURAL) ——————————————

PLURAL NOUN ——————————————

ADJECTIVE ——————————————

PLURAL NOUN ——————————————

ADJECTIVE ——————————————

NOUN ——————————————

ADJECTIVE ——————————————

ADJECTIVE ——————————————

NOUN ——————————————

PLURAL NOUN ——————————————

NOUN ——————————————

EXCLAMATION ——————————————

DECORATING THE TREE

Many people decorate their Christmas tree on Christmas Eve. Last

year _____ had a party and everyone helped _____
     PERSON IN ROOM   VERB

the tree. _____ brought tinsel and _____. And
      PERSON IN ROOM   PLURAL NOUN

_____ brought lots of fresh _____ and
  PERSON IN ROOM   TYPE OF FOOD (PLURAL)

candy _____ to put on the tree. The most important
      TYPE OF FOOD (PLURAL)

decoration, of course, is the string of colored electric _____.
                                              PLURAL NOUN

A few dozen lights make any tree look _____. And most
                                  ADJECTIVE

stores sell round, sparkly _____ and little _____
                    PLURAL NOUN   ADJECTIVE

balls to hang on the branches. But the hardest decoration to pick is the

one that goes right on top. Once that _____ is up, you know
                                   NOUN

that the _____ season has officially started. Of course, if
          ADJECTIVE

you are too _____ to have a tree for Christmas, you can
           ADJECTIVE

decorate your _____ or hang _____ on your
              NOUN   PLURAL NOUN

_____. Then the neighbors will say, "_____!"
  NOUN   EXCLAMATION

From CHRISTMAS FUN MAD LIBS® • Copyright © 2001, 1985 by Penguin Random House LLC.

MAD LIBS® is fun to play with friends, but you can also play it by yourself! To begin with, DO NOT look at the story on the page below. Fill in the blanks on this page with the words called for. Then, using the words you have selected, fill in the blank spaces in the story.

Now you've created your own hilarious MAD LIBS® game!

HOW TO WRAP A PRESENT

ADJECTIVE _____

PLURAL NOUN _____

ADJECTIVE _____

NOUN _____

PLURAL NOUN _____

VERB _____

NOUN _____

ADVERB _____

NOUN _____

COLOR _____

NOUN _____

ADJECTIVE _____

VERB _____

ADJECTIVE _____

PLURAL NOUN _____

ADJECTIVE _____

EXCLAMATION _____

ADJECTIVE _____

HOW TO WRAP
A PRESENT

Before you start to wrap your Christmas present, make sure you have

plenty of _____ paper and lots of little _____ to
          ADJECTIVE   PLURAL NOUN

stick on the package. If you are wrapping something _____,
                                             ADJECTIVE

such as a/an _____, it is best to tape _____
             NOUN   PLURAL NOUN

around any parts that might _____. Then take brown
                             VERB

wrapping _____ and wrap it very _____. Take
          NOUN   ADVERB

care that there is not a/an _____ poking out anywhere.
                            NOUN

Now take the expensive _____ paper that you bought at
                       COLOR

the _____ store and make a/an _____ package.
      NOUN   ADJECTIVE

Finally, put stickers on that say "Do not _____ until
                                      VERB

Christmas" and put it under the tree with all the other _____
                                                ADJECTIVE

_____. Then on Christmas morning, when you see all
PLURAL NOUN

your _____ relatives opening their packages and saying,
     ADJECTIVE

"_____!" you will feel positively _____.
    EXCLAMATION   ADJECTIVE

From CHRISTMAS FUN MAD LIBS® • Copyright © 2001, 1985 by Penguin Random House LLC.

WHAT TO GET PEOPLE FOR CHRISTMAS

ADJECTIVE _____

PLURAL NOUN _____

NOUN _____

NOUN _____

ADJECTIVE _____

NOUN _____

VERB _____

NOUN _____

A PLACE _____

VERB _____

PLURAL NOUN _____

PERSON IN ROOM _____

ARTICLE OF CLOTHING _____

CELEBRITY _____

PERSON IN ROOM _____

PLURAL NOUN _____

PART OF THE BODY _____

NOUN _____

MAD LIBS® is fun to play with friends, but you can also play it by yourself! To begin with, DO NOT look at the story on the page below. Fill in the blanks on this page with the words called for. Then, using the words you have selected, fill in the blank spaces in the story.

Now you've created your own hilarious MAD LIBS® game!

WHAT TO GET PEOPLE FOR CHRISTMAS

One of the best things about Christmas is being able to pick out

_____ presents to give to your _____ and
    ADJECTIVE   PLURAL NOUN

relatives. But it's a problem because you don't want to give someone

a/an _____ when they really wanted a/an _____.
        NOUN   NOUN

Here are some _____ gift ideas. I bet your mother would
                     ADJECTIVE

like a new electric _____ she could use to _____
                  NOUN   VERB

her vegetables or clean the _____ in (the) _____.
                        NOUN   A PLACE

If your father likes to _____, he could use a new set of
                     VERB

_____. If you want to get _____
PLURAL NOUN   PERSON IN ROOM

a present, she needs a sports _____ designed
                        ARTICLE OF CLOTHING

by _____. And _____ needs some
   CELEBRITY   PERSON IN ROOM

_____ to keep his _____ warm. But no matter
PLURAL NOUN   PART OF THE BODY

what you give, remember it is the _____ behind the gift that
                                NOUN

counts.

From CHRISTMAS FUN MAD LIBS® • Copyright © 2001, 1985 by Penguin Random House LLC.

CHRISTMAS DINNER

ADJECTIVE _____

NOUN _____

TYPE OF FOOD _____

PLURAL NOUN _____

TYPE OF LIQUID _____

ADJECTIVE _____

VERB _____

NOUN _____

PART OF THE BODY _____

NOUN _____

ADJECTIVE _____

NOUN _____

NUMBER _____

ADVERB _____

ADJECTIVE _____

PLURAL NOUN _____

EXCLAMATION _____

MAD LIBS® is fun to play with friends, but you can also play it by yourself! To begin with, DO NOT look at the story on the page below. Fill in the blanks on this page with the words called for. Then, using the words you have selected, fill in the blank spaces in the story.

Now you've created your own hilarious MAD LIBS® game!

CHRISTMAS DINNER

Everyone likes to have a/an _____ dinner on Christmas Day.
                            ADJECTIVE

Most people have a huge roast _____ stuffed with
                                       NOUN

_____ dressing and served with mashed _____
TYPE OF FOOD   PLURAL NOUN

and plenty of hot brown _____. However, if you would
                     TYPE OF LIQUID

rather have a/an _____ turkey, here is how you should
                ADJECTIVE

_____ it. First, make the dressing of old, dried _____
    VERB   NOUN

crumbs. Then, put the dressing in the turkey's _____. Put it
                                 PART OF THE BODY

in a big _____ and brush it with _____ butter. Next,
       NOUN   ADJECTIVE

heat your _____ to _____ degrees. Put the turkey in
        NOUN   NUMBER

and cook it very _____ for five hours. When you put it on the
               ADVERB

table, the _____ aroma will make everyone smack their
             ADJECTIVE

_____ and say, "_____!"
PLURAL NOUN   EXCLAMATION

From CHRISTMAS FUN MAD LIBS® • Copyright © 2001, 1985 by Penguin Random House LLC.

TOYS FOR THE KIDS

_____ ADJECTIVE

_____ PLURAL NOUN

_____ ADJECTIVE

_____ SILLY WORD

_____ PLURAL NOUN

_____ NUMBER

_____ VERB

_____ LETTER OF THE ALPHABET

_____ PLURAL NOUN

_____ NOUN

_____ ANIMAL

_____ NOUN

_____ NOUN

_____ ADJECTIVE

_____ ADJECTIVE

_____ ADJECTIVE

_____ PLURAL NOUN

MAD LIBS® is fun to play with friends, but you can also play it by yourself! To begin with, DO NOT look at the story on the page below. Fill in the blanks on this page with the words called for. Then, using the words you have selected, fill in the blank spaces in the story.

Now you've created your own hilarious MAD LIBS® game!

TOYS FOR THE KIDS

Today's parents buy very _____ toys for their little
                              ADJECTIVE

_____. Fifty years ago, children got _____
     PLURAL NOUN   ADJECTIVE

electric trains or baby dolls that said, "_____" when you
                                              SILLY WORD

squeezed them. Now children only want electronic _____.
                                                      PLURAL NOUN

Even _____-year-olds know how to _____ a computer.
         NUMBER   VERB

Or a/an _____ -Phone. Kids want remote-controlled
        LETTER OF THE ALPHABET

_____. Or tiny robot monsters that can blow up your
   PLURAL NOUN

_____ or take your _____ prisoner. Everything
      NOUN   ANIMAL

has to have a silicon _____ in it and be operated by a nine-
                            NOUN

volt _____. By the year 2030, all American children will
         NOUN

probably want to have their own _____ space shuttle and
                                      ADJECTIVE

_____ robot playmate manufactured by General
     ADJECTIVE

Motors. In fact, by that time maybe children will be manufactured by

a/an _____ assembly line and will be operated by nine-volt
        ADJECTIVE

_____.
   PLURAL NOUN

From CHRISTMAS FUN MAD LIBS® • Copyright © 2001, 1985 by Penguin Random House LLC.

MAD LIBS® is fun to play with friends, but you can also play it by yourself! To begin with, DO NOT look at the story on the page below. Fill in the blanks on this page with the words called for. Then, using the words you have selected, fill in the blank spaces in the story.

Now you've created your own hilarious MAD LIBS® game!

DEAR SANTA

PERSON IN ROOM _____

NOUN _____

ADJECTIVE _____

VERB _____

EXCLAMATION _____

VERB (PAST TENSE) _____

VERB (PAST TENSE) _____

PLURAL NOUN _____

ADJECTIVE _____

NOUN _____

ADJECTIVE _____

NOUN _____

PERSON IN ROOM _____

ADJECTIVE _____

ADJECTIVE _____

ARTICLE OF CLOTHING _____

DEAR SANTA

Dear Santa,

My name is _____, and all year I have been a very, very
                   PERSON IN ROOM

good _____. I have been _____ at school, and
            NOUN   ADJECTIVE

when my teacher asked me to _____ the whiteboard, I
                                   VERB

just said, "_____!" I have not _____
              EXCLAMATION   VERB (PAST TENSE)

or _____. Not even once. And I have helped a lot
      VERB (PAST TENSE)

of old _____ cross the street. Because I have been so
          PLURAL NOUN

_____, I am sure you are going to bring me a brand-new
      ADJECTIVE

_____ with _____ wheels. I would also like to
      NOUN   ADJECTIVE

have a/an _____ racket. And a secret microphone so I can
               NOUN

spy on _____ and learn all his/her _____ secrets.
          PERSON IN ROOM   ADJECTIVE

Well, Santa, I know you will put all these _____ presents in
                                                ADJECTIVE

my _____ on Christmas. Or else I will have been
      ARTICLE OF CLOTHING

good for nothing.

From CHRISTMAS FUN MAD LIBS® • Copyright © 2001, 1985 by Penguin Random House LLC.

MAD LIBS® is fun to play with friends, but you can also play it by yourself! To begin with, DO NOT look at the story on the page below. Fill in the blanks on this page with the words called for. Then, using the words you have selected, fill in the blank spaces in the story.

Now you've created your own hilarious MAD LIBS® game!

A VISIT WITH SANTA AT THE NORTH POLE

ADJECTIVE _____

PLURAL NOUN _____

FIRST NAME _____

ADJECTIVE _____

NUMBER _____

PLURAL NOUN _____

PLURAL NOUN _____

VEHICLE _____

ADJECTIVE _____

ANIMAL (PLURAL) _____

NOUN _____

NOUN _____

ARTICLE OF CLOTHING (PLURAL) _____

NUMBER _____

VERB _____

A VISIT WITH SANTA
AT THE NORTH POLE

Santa Claus has a very _____ life. He lives at the North
                              ADJECTIVE

Pole surrounded by snow and _____. He is married
                                 PLURAL NOUN

to _____ Claus and instead of children, they have
      FIRST NAME

_____ little elves. This way, Santa can get help in his workshop
ADJECTIVE

for only _____ dollars an hour. The elves work eleven months
          NUMBER

a year making _____ and _____ for Santa
                 PLURAL NOUN   PLURAL NOUN

to give children on Christmas. On Christmas Eve, the elves load up

Santa's _____ with the _____ presents. Then Santa
            VEHICLE   ADJECTIVE

hitches it to his team of _____ and goes sailing through
                          ANIMAL (PLURAL)

the sky. When he sees a child's house, he lands on the _____
                                                          NOUN

and slides down the chimney, landing on the _____. Then
                                                NOUN

he puts the presents into the _____ that the
                              ARTICLE OF CLOTHING (PLURAL)

children have hung on the mantelpiece. After he does this _____
                                                           NUMBER

times, he goes home to get ready to _____.
                                     VERB

From CHRISTMAS FUN MAD LIBS® • Copyright © 2001, 1985 by Penguin Random House LLC.

MAD LIBS® is fun to play with friends, but you can also play it by yourself! To begin with, DO NOT look at the story on the page below. Fill in the blanks on this page with the words called for. Then, using the words you have selected, fill in the blank spaces in the story.

Now you've created your own hilarious MAD LIBS® game!

GOING TO SEE SANTA

PERSON IN ROOM _____

NUMBER _____

PART OF THE BODY _____

NOUN _____

NOUN _____

ADJECTIVE _____

NOUN _____

ADJECTIVE _____

COLOR _____

ARTICLE OF CLOTHING (PLURAL) _____

NOUN _____

SILLY WORD _____

NOUN _____

EXCLAMATION _____

ANIMAL _____

NOUN _____

PLURAL NOUN _____

ADVERB _____

GOING TO SEE SANTA

Yesterday, I took my friend _____ to see Santa Claus at the
PERSON IN ROOM

department store. He/She is only _____ years old, so I had to
NUMBER

be sure to hold on to his/her _____ whenever we crossed
PART OF THE BODY

a/an _____. When we got to the _____, there
NOUN   NOUN

was a long line of _____ kids waiting to talk to Santa, who
ADJECTIVE

was sitting on a platform in the _____ department. Santa
NOUN

Claus is a big, fat, _____ man with a/an _____
ADJECTIVE   COLOR

beard who dresses in bright red _____.
ARTICLE OF CLOTHING (PLURAL)

Whenever a little kid came up, Santa would sit the child on his

_____ and say, "_____." Then he would say,
NOUN   SILLY WORD

"Now, have you been a good little _____?" And the kid
NOUN

would say, "_____!" Then Santa would say, "And what
EXCLAMATION

do you want for Christmas?" And the kid would say, "I want a/an

_____," or "I want an electric _____," or "I want
ANIMAL   NOUN

some little toy _____." Then Santa would say, "You bet,"
PLURAL NOUN

and the kid would run _____ back to his or her parents.
ADVERB

From CHRISTMAS FUN MAD LIBS® • Copyright © 2001, 1985 by Penguin Random House LLC.

MAD LIBS® is fun to play with friends, but you can also play it by yourself! To begin with, DO NOT look at the story on the page below. Fill in the blanks on this page with the words called for. Then, using the words you have selected, fill in the blank spaces in the story.

Now you've created your own hilarious MAD LIBS® game!

THE TWELVE DAYS OF CHRISTMAS

_____ NOUN

_____ NOUN

_____ ADJECTIVE

_____ NOUN

_____ ANIMAL (PLURAL)

_____ NOUN

_____ NUMBER

_____ ADJECTIVE

_____ PLURAL NOUN

_____ PLURAL NOUN

_____ NOUN

_____ PLURAL NOUN

_____ ADJECTIVE

_____ NOUN

THE TWELVE DAYS
OF CHRISTMAS

On the first day of Christmas, my true love gave to me a/an

_____ in a/an _____ tree. On the second day of
　　　NOUN　　　　　　　　　　　NOUN

Christmas, my true love gave to me two _____ doves and
　　　　　　　　　　　　　　　　　　ADJECTIVE

a/an _____ in a pear tree. On the third day of Christmas, my
　　　　NOUN

true love gave to me three French _____, two turtle
　　　　　　　　　　　　　　　　ANIMAL (PLURAL)

doves, and a/an _____ in a pear tree. On the fourth day of
　　　　　　　　　NOUN

Christmas, my true love gave to me _____ _____
　　　　　　　　　　　　　　　　　　NUMBER　　　ADJECTIVE

_____, three French _____, two turtle
　PLURAL NOUN　　　　　　　　　PLURAL NOUN

doves, and a/an _____ in a pear tree. On the fifth day of
　　　　　　　　NOUN

Christmas, my true love gave to me five golden _____,
　　　　　　　　　　　　　　　　　　　　　　PLURAL NOUN

four calling birds, three _____ hens, two turtle doves, and
　　　　　　　　　　　ADJECTIVE

a/an _____ in a pear tree.
　　　　NOUN

From CHRISTMAS FUN MAD LIBS® • Copyright © 2001, 1985 by Penguin Random House LLC.

MAD LIBS® is fun to play with friends, but you can also play it by yourself! To begin with, DO NOT look at the story on the page below. Fill in the blanks on this page with the words called for. Then, using the words you have selected, fill in the blank spaces in the story.

Now you've created your own hilarious MAD LIBS® game!

CHRISTMAS CAROLS

ADJECTIVE _____

ADJECTIVE _____

ADVERB _____

PLURAL NOUN _____

SILLY WORD (PLURAL) _____

PLURAL NOUN _____

NOUN _____

COLOR _____

A PLACE _____

PLURAL NOUN _____

OCCUPATION (PLURAL) _____

ADJECTIVE _____

PLURAL NOUN _____

CITY _____

A PLACE _____

NUMBER _____

PERSON IN ROOM _____

Christmas Cheer MAD LIBS®

CHRISTMAS CAROLS

This Christmas, our _____ glee club is planning a/an
ADJECTIVE

_____ program of Christmas carols. We all sing very
ADJECTIVE

_____ and are going to sing on the streets and collect
ADVERB

_____ to feed the poor, hungry _____ in
PLURAL NOUN   SILLY WORD (PLURAL)

Transylvania. Our program will start with "Jingle _____,"
PLURAL NOUN

followed by "Rudolph, the Red-Nosed _____," "I'm
NOUN

Dreaming of a/an _____ Christmas," and "Santa Claus
COLOR

Is Coming to (the) _____." My favorites, however, are
A PLACE

"Deck the Halls with Boughs of _____," "We Three
PLURAL NOUN

_____ of Orient Are," and "Walking in a/an
OCCUPATION (PLURAL)

_____ Wonderland." If it goes well, we can form a group, call
ADJECTIVE

ourselves the _____, and do concerts in _____
PLURAL NOUN   CITY

or even in (the) _____. We'll have _____ fans and
A PLACE   NUMBER

make a video. We'll be as famous as _____.
PERSON IN ROOM

From CHRISTMAS FUN MAD LIBS® • Copyright © 2001, 1985 by Penguin Random House LLC.

A TRANSYLVANIAN NEW YEAR'S

ADJECTIVE _____

NOUN _____

NOUN _____

PLURAL NOUN _____

PLURAL NOUN _____

ADVERB _____

PLURAL NOUN _____

ADJECTIVE _____

ANIMAL _____

TYPE OF FOOD _____

NUMBER _____

VERB _____

SILLY WORD _____

NUMBER _____

PLURAL NOUN _____

NOUN _____

ADJECTIVE _____

MAD LIBS® is fun to play with friends, but you can also play it by yourself! To begin with, DO NOT look at the story on the page below. Fill in the blanks on this page with the words called for. Then, using the words you have selected, fill in the blank spaces in the story.

Now you've created your own hilarious MAD LIBS® game!

A TRANSYLVANIAN NEW YEAR'S

New Year's Day in Transylvania is the most _____ holiday
ADJECTIVE
of the year. All the _____ shops and _____
NOUN   NOUN
factories are shut down, and the _____ dance in the
PLURAL NOUN
streets. The locals, who are called _____, spend all day
PLURAL NOUN
dancing _____. And some Transylvanians, who are called
ADVERB
_____, prepare a/an _____ feast. New Year's
PLURAL NOUN   ADJECTIVE
dinner always features a wild roast _____. It is skinned,
ANIMAL
put in an oven, and covered with _____. Then it is cooked
TYPE OF FOOD
for _____ hours. After dinner, a contest is held to see which
NUMBER
Transylvanian can _____ the loudest. The winner is
VERB
given the title of "_____." Then, famous Count Dracula
SILLY WORD
himself raffles off _____ _____ to help pay the
NUMBER   PLURAL NOUN
_____ who has to come in the next day and clean up the
NOUN
whole _____ country.
ADJECTIVE

From CHRISTMAS FUN MAD LIBS® • Copyright © 2001, 1985 by Penguin Random House LLC.

NEW YEAR'S RESOLUTION

NOUN _____

NOUN _____

VERB _____

TYPE OF FOOD _____

PLURAL NOUN _____

PLURAL NOUN _____

ADJECTIVE _____

PLURAL NOUN _____

VERB _____

TYPE OF LIQUID _____

PART OF THE BODY _____

ARTICLE OF CLOTHING _____

ADJECTIVE _____

ADVERB _____

ADJECTIVE _____

MAD LIBS® is fun to play with friends, but you can also play it by yourself! To begin with, DO NOT look at the story on the page below. Fill in the blanks on this page with the words called for. Then, using the words you have selected, fill in the blank spaces in the story.

Now you've created your own hilarious MAD LIBS® game!

NEW YEAR'S RESOLUTION

I resolve that in the next year I will eat all my _____, just
                                                        NOUN

like my mother says. I promise to help bathe my pet _____
                                                              NOUN

and help _____ the dishes after dinner. I will not eat any
               VERB

_____ that contains cholesterol or _____. I
   TYPE OF FOOD   PLURAL NOUN

will be polite and thoughtful and will clear the _____
                                                        PLURAL NOUN

after meals. I will do a/an _____ deed every day. I will also
                                  ADJECTIVE

be polite to any _____ who are older than I am. And I
                       PLURAL NOUN

will never, never _____ my dog's tail or pour _____
                         VERB   TYPE OF LIQUID

on my cat. I will also try to brush my _____ and shine
                                              PART OF THE BODY

my _____ every day. I promise to be really
        ARTICLE OF CLOTHING

_____ so I can live _____ for the next twelve
   ADJECTIVE   ADVERB

months. Then I'll be a truly happy, _____ person.
                                          ADJECTIVE

From CHRISTMAS FUN MAD LIBS® • Copyright © 2001, 1985 by Penguin Random House LLC.

MAD LIBS® is fun to play with friends, but you can also play it by yourself! To begin with, DO NOT look at the story on the page below. Fill in the blanks on this page with the words called for. Then, using the words you have selected, fill in the blank spaces in the story.

Now you've created your own hilarious MAD LIBS® game!

SCROOGE

PERSON IN ROOM ————————————

COUNTRY ——————————

NOUN ——————————

PLURAL NOUN ——————————

NUMBER ——————————

SILLY WORD ——————————

ADJECTIVE ——————————

NUMBER ——————————

NOUN ——————————

NOUN ——————————

ADJECTIVE ——————————

NUMBER ——————————

ADJECTIVE ——————————

ADJECTIVE ——————————

NOUN ——————————

FIRST NAME ——————————

COLOR ——————————

EXCLAMATION ——————————

SCROOGE

You have just read *A Christmas Carol* by _____. Years ago in
_____PERSON IN ROOM

London, _____, lived a mean, stingy _____
_____COUNTRY_____NOUN

named Scrooge. He was so stingy, he saved _____. In
_____PLURAL NOUN

fact, he had more than _____ of them. When anyone mentioned
_____NUMBER

Christmas, Scrooge said, "Bah! _____." He had a/an
_____SILLY WORD

_____ bookkeeper named Bob Cratchit, and Scrooge made
____ADJECTIVE

him work _____ hours a day. One Christmas Eve, Mr. Scrooge
_____NUMBER

had a dream. He saw the Ghost of Christmas Past, who showed him

what a/an _____ _____ he had been. Then the
_____ADJECTIVE_____NOUN

_____ of Christmas Present showed Scrooge the miserable
____NOUN

home of Bob Cratchit and poor Tiny Tim. Tiny Tim had a temperature

of _____ degrees. Then Scrooge met the Ghost of Christmas
____NUMBER

_____, who took him to a/an _____ cemetery,
____ADJECTIVE_____ADJECTIVE

where Scrooge saw his own _____. He also saw the grave
_____NOUN

of Tiny _____. Scrooge turned _____ and
_____FIRST NAME_____COLOR

shouted, "_____!"
_____EXCLAMATION

From CHRISTMAS FUN MAD LIBS® • Copyright © 2001, 1985 by Penguin Random House LLC.

SCROOGE (CONTINUED)

NOUN _____

NOUN _____

NOUN _____

NOUN _____

ARTICLE OF CLOTHING _____

ANIMAL _____

ADJECTIVE _____

NOUN _____

NOUN _____

NOUN _____

ADJECTIVE _____

PLURAL NOUN _____

ADJECTIVE _____

PLURAL NOUN _____

ADJECTIVE _____

NOUN _____

NOUN _____

CELEBRITY _____

MAD LIBS® is fun to play with friends, but you can also play it by yourself! To begin with, DO NOT look at the story on the page below. Fill in the blanks on this page with the words called for. Then, using the words you have selected, fill in the blank spaces in the story.

Now you've created your own hilarious MAD LIBS® game!

SCROOGE (CONTINUED)

The next morning when the _____ came up, Scrooge jumped
                          NOUN
out of his _____ and said, "I am a changed _____.
           NOUN   NOUN
I only hope it is not too late for me to become a kindly, generous

_____." He put on his _____, rushed
   NOUN   ARTICLE OF CLOTHING
to the butcher shop, and said, "Give me the biggest _____
                                                      ANIMAL
you have." Then he bought cakes and _____ cookies and
                                     ADJECTIVE
a beautiful _____ pudding. He put everything in a big
             NOUN
_____, rushed to Bob Cratchit's house, and pounded on
   NOUN
the _____. When Bob Cratchit opened the door, Scrooge
     NOUN
said, "_____ Christmas, Bob. I have _____ for
        ADJECTIVE   PLURAL NOUN
everyone, including Tiny Tim." And they all had a/an _____
                                                      ADJECTIVE
dinner and sang jolly _____. Scrooge had indeed changed
                       PLURAL NOUN
from a/an _____ skinflint into a wonderful _____.
           ADJECTIVE   NOUN
He gave Tiny Tim a solid gold _____, and Tiny Tim said,
                               NOUN
"Merry Christmas, and may _____ bless us, every one . . ."
                           CELEBRITY

From CHRISTMAS FUN MAD LIBS® • Copyright © 2001, 1985 by Penguin Random House LLC.

MAD LIBS® is fun to play with friends, but you can also play it by yourself! To begin with, DO NOT look at the story on the page below. Fill in the blanks on this page with the words called for. Then, using the words you have selected, fill in the blank spaces in the story.

Now you've created your own hilarious MAD LIBS® game!

THE SCHOOL PARTY

_____ ADJECTIVE

_____ NOUN

_____ PERSON IN ROOM

_____ NOUN

_____ NOUN

_____ PERSON IN ROOM

_____ CELEBRITY

_____ NOUN

_____ PLURAL NOUN

_____ PERSON IN ROOM

_____ ADJECTIVE

_____ TYPE OF FOOD

_____ TYPE OF LIQUID

_____ ADJECTIVE

_____ NUMBER

_____ PLURAL NOUN

_____ PERSON IN ROOM

_____ EXCLAMATION

THE SCHOOL PARTY

We had a/an _____ Christmas party at school last year.
            ADJECTIVE

Our _____ teacher, _____, let us use the
        NOUN   PERSON IN ROOM

_____ room. And my favorite _____ teacher,
    NOUN   NOUN

_____, was in charge of the decorations. We all drew
PERSON IN ROOM

pictures of _____ on colored paper and hung them
              CELEBRITY

on a long _____. Then we cut out stars, snowflakes,
              NOUN

and _____ and pasted them on the windows. Then
      PLURAL NOUN

_____, who is my math teacher, made the _____
PERSON IN ROOM   ADJECTIVE

refreshments. We had burgers and _____ and cups of hot
                                    TYPE OF FOOD

_____. Our principal bought a really _____
TYPE OF LIQUID   ADJECTIVE

tree that was _____ feet tall. And everyone put their
                  NUMBER

_____ under it. _____ dressed up like Santa
PLURAL NOUN   PERSON IN ROOM

Claus and said, "_____!"
                  EXCLAMATION

From CHRISTMAS FUN MAD LIBS® • Copyright © 2001, 1985 by Penguin Random House LLC.

MAD LIBS® is fun to play with friends, but you can also play it by yourself! To begin with, DO NOT look at the story on the page below. Fill in the blanks on this page with the words called for. Then, using the words you have selected, fill in the blank spaces in the story.

Now you've created your own hilarious MAD LIBS® game!

THANK-YOU LETTERS

_____ FIRST NAME

_____ ADJECTIVE

_____ NOUN

_____ PLURAL NOUN

_____ PART OF THE BODY

_____ ADJECTIVE

_____ ADJECTIVE

_____ FIRST NAME

_____ NOUN

_____ PLURAL NOUN

_____ ADJECTIVE

_____ PLURAL NOUN

_____ ADJECTIVE

_____ PLURAL NOUN

_____ NOUN

_____ CELEBRITY

THANK-YOU LETTERS

Dear Auntie _____,
                   FIRST NAME

I want to thank you for sending me the _____ gift. I never
                                            ADJECTIVE

had a/an _____ before. I can use it to fix all my
              NOUN

_____. It will also keep my _____ warm if we
   PLURAL NOUN   PART OF THE BODY

have any _____ weather.
             ADJECTIVE

Your _____ nephew,
         ADJECTIVE

_____
   FIRST NAME

Dear Grandpa and Grandma,

I really like the _____ you sent me. It must have cost a lot of
                     NOUN

_____. All the kids around here have _____
   PLURAL NOUN   ADJECTIVE

computers. But mine is the only one that has six different

_____. It will help me do my _____ homework,
   PLURAL NOUN   ADJECTIVE

and I know I will get higher _____ this year. Mom says I
                               PLURAL NOUN

can come to your _____ for a visit next summer.
                      NOUN

Signed,

_____
   CELEBRITY

From CHRISTMAS FUN MAD LIBS® • Copyright © 2001, 1985 by Penguin Random House LLC.

HOLIDAY TRAVELING

PLURAL NOUN ——————————————

PLURAL NOUN ——————————————

ADJECTIVE ——————————————

NOUN ——————————————

PLURAL NOUN ——————————————

ADJECTIVE ——————————————

A PLACE ——————————————

A PLACE ——————————————

NUMBER ——————————————

PLURAL NOUN ——————————————

NUMBER ——————————————

PLURAL NOUN ——————————————

PART OF THE BODY ——————————————

ADJECTIVE ——————————————

PLURAL NOUN ——————————————

PLURAL NOUN ——————————————

MAD LIBS® is fun to play with friends, but you can also play it by yourself! To begin with, DO NOT look at the story on the page below. Fill in the blanks on this page with the words called for. Then, using the words you have selected, fill in the blank spaces in the story.

Now you've created your own hilarious MAD LIBS® game!

HOLIDAY TRAVELING

During the holidays, more _____ go back home to
                          PLURAL NOUN
visit their _____ than at any other time. Between
            PLURAL NOUN
Christmas and _____ Year's Day, the airlines pack the
                 ADJECTIVE
_____ in like sardines in a/an _____. There
   PLURAL NOUN   NOUN
are a lot of _____ "no frill" airlines that will take you from
              ADJECTIVE
(the) _____ to (the) _____ for only _____
       A PLACE   A PLACE   NUMBER
dollars. These airlines do not give you any _____. And
                                               PLURAL NOUN
you can only take _____ pieces of luggage. They also have
                     NUMBER
smaller _____, and you often have to sit on someone
          PLURAL NOUN
else's _____. It is very _____ to travel during the
        PART OF THE BODY   ADJECTIVE
holidays, but it is worth it to make your _____ happy.
                                            PLURAL NOUN
Don't forget to make your _____ early.
                             PLURAL NOUN

From CHRISTMAS FUN MAD LIBS® • Copyright © 2001, 1985 by Penguin Random House LLC.

NEW YEAR'S BOWL GAMES

CITY _____

ANIMAL (PLURAL) _____

A PLACE _____

ANIMAL (PLURAL) _____

NOUN _____

CITY _____

ANIMAL (PLURAL) _____

CITY _____

PLURAL NOUN _____

ANIMAL _____

TYPE OF FOOD _____

CITY _____

CITY _____

ANIMAL (PLURAL) _____

NOUN _____

PERSON IN ROOM _____

NOUN _____

COLOR _____

MAD LIBS® is fun to play with friends, but you can also play it by yourself! To begin with, DO NOT look at the story on the page below. Fill in the blanks on this page with the words called for. Then, using the words you have selected, fill in the blank spaces in the story.

Now you've created your own hilarious MAD LIBS® game!

NEW YEAR'S
BOWL GAMES

On New Year's Day, there are always a lot of football games. On
television, they interrupt the game with commercials every few
minutes. This year the _____ _____ are
                              CITY   ANIMAL (PLURAL)
playing the _____ _____ in the famous
                A PLACE   ANIMAL (PLURAL)
_____ Bowl. And the _____ _____
    NOUN   CITY   ANIMAL (PLURAL)
are matched up against the nation's number one team, the _____
                                                              CITY
_____. They will be playing in the _____ Bowl.
    PLURAL NOUN   ANIMAL
But the game that everyone is talking about is the _____
                                                        TYPE OF FOOD
Bowl. There, the _____ Cowboys will play the hard-
                        CITY
hitting _____ _____, whose quarterback is
            CITY   ANIMAL (PLURAL)
the super-_____, _____. They will play in
                NOUN   PERSON IN ROOM
the fabulous Houston Astro-_____, which has a sliding roof
                                NOUN
and _____ AstroTurf.
        COLOR

From CHRISTMAS FUN MAD LIBS® • Copyright © 2001, 1985 by Penguin Random House LLC.

MAD LIBS® is fun to play with friends, but you can also play it by yourself! To begin with, DO NOT look at the story on the page below. Fill in the blanks on this page with the words called for. Then, using the words you have selected, fill in the blank spaces in the story.

Now you've created your own hilarious MAD LIBS® game!

CHRISTMAS VACATION

_____ ADJECTIVE

_____ ADJECTIVE

_____ ADJECTIVE

_____ NOUN

_____ NOUN

_____ NOUN

_____ NOUN

_____ ADJECTIVE

_____ VERB

_____ NOUN

_____ PLURAL NOUN

_____ NOUN

_____ PLURAL NOUN

_____ NOUN

_____ PLURAL NOUN

_____ NOUN

_____ A PLACE

_____ COLOR

CHRISTMAS VACATION

This year my entire family—my sister, my _____ brother, and
                                              ADJECTIVE
my parents—are planning to spend the holidays in the _____
                                                          ADJECTIVE
mountains in a/an _____ cabin built by my _____.
                      ADJECTIVE   NOUN
The cabin is in the middle of a huge _____ on the edge
                                            NOUN
of a/an _____, which is always frozen at this time of the
              NOUN
_____. If the ice is _____ enough, we will be able to
    NOUN   ADJECTIVE
_____ on it. We will decorate the big pine _____
    VERB   NOUN
in front of the cabin with Christmas _____. At night, we
                                          PLURAL NOUN
will build a fire in the _____ and toast _____.
                              NOUN   PLURAL NOUN
It promises to be a great _____. Next year I hope we can
                                NOUN
save up enough _____ so that we can afford to get on
                    PLURAL NOUN
a/an _____ and fly to (the) _____ and have a
          NOUN   A PLACE
really _____ Christmas.
            COLOR

From CHRISTMAS FUN MAD LIBS® • Copyright © 2001, 1985 by Penguin Random House LLC.

THE NIGHT BEFORE CHRISTMAS

NOUN _____

ANIMAL _____

ANIMAL _____

PLURAL NOUN _____

TYPE OF FOOD (PLURAL) _____

PART OF THE BODY (PLURAL) _____

NOUN _____

NOUN _____

PERSON IN ROOM _____

VEHICLE _____

NUMBER _____

ANIMAL (PLURAL) _____

PLURAL NOUN _____

PART OF THE BODY _____

PART OF THE BODY _____

VERB (PAST TENSE) _____

VERB (PAST TENSE) _____

ADJECTIVE _____

MAD LIBS® is fun to play with friends, but you can also play it by yourself! To begin with, DO NOT look at the story on the page below. Fill in the blanks on this page with the words called for. Then, using the words you have selected, fill in the blank spaces in the story.

Now you've created your own hilarious MAD LIBS® game!

THE NIGHT BEFORE CHRISTMAS

'Twas the night before Christmas and all through the _____,

NOUN

not a/an _____ was stirring, not even a/an _____.

ANIMAL   ANIMAL

The children were nestled all snug in their _____,

PLURAL NOUN

while visions of _____ danced in their

TYPE OF FOOD (PLURAL)

_____. When out on the lawn there arose such a

PART OF THE BODY (PLURAL)

clatter, I sprang from my _____ to see what was the matter.

NOUN

I knew in a/an _____ it must be Saint _____,

NOUN   PERSON IN ROOM

with his miniature _____ and _____ tiny

VEHICLE   NUMBER

_____. He filled all our _____, then

ANIMAL (PLURAL)   PLURAL NOUN

laying his _____ aside of his _____, up the

PART OF THE BODY   PART OF THE BODY

chimney he _____. But I heard him exclaim, as he

VERB (PAST TENSE)

_____ out of sight, "Merry Christmas to all and to

VERB (PAST TENSE)

all a/an _____ night."

ADJECTIVE

From CHRISTMAS FUN MAD LIBS® • Copyright © 2001, 1985 by Penguin Random House LLC.

Download Mad Libs today!

Join the millions of Mad Libs fans
creating wacky and wonderful
stories on our apps!